FOCUS ON SUCCESS

The new edition

Allgemeine Ausgabe

David Clarke
Michael Macfarlane

Cornelsen

Focus on Success – The new edition: Allgemeine Ausgabe wurde geplant und entwickelt von der Redaktion Moderne Fremdsprachen des Cornelsen Verlags, Berlin.

Verfasser:	David Clarke, Witten Michael Macfarlane, Oxford
Berater:	Rolf Bastian, Wetzlar Philipp Fehrenbach, Nürtingen Elke Uthoff, Osnabrück Sibylle Vogel, Erfurt Sybille Weiß, Mönchengladbach Kathrin Wendling, Kamenz
Projektleitung:	Jim Austin
Verlagsredaktion:	Andreas Goebel
Außenredaktion:	Christine House
Redaktionelle Mitarbeit:	Leah Holroyd, Laura Spratling Oliver Busch (Wörterverzeichnisse)
Bildredaktion:	Gertha Maly
Layout und technische Umsetzung:	Petra Eberhard Grafik Design, Berlin
Umschlaggestaltung:	werkstatt für gebrauchsgrafik, Berlin
Illustrationen:	Oxford Designers & Illustrators

www.cornelsen.de

1. Auflage, 1. Druck 2008

Alle Drucke dieser Auflage sind inhaltlich unverändert und können im Unterricht nebeneinander verwendet werden.

Druck: CS-Druck CornelsenStürtz, Berlin

ISBN 978-3-06-020227-0

Inhalt gedruckt auf säurefreiem Papier aus nachhaltiger Forstwirtschaft.

VORWORT

Liebe Lehrerinnen und Lehrer,

Focus on Success – The new edition: Allgemeine Ausgabe ist konzipiert für Lernende an Fachoberschulen und Berufskollegs. Es setzt Englischkenntnisse auf dem Niveau des mittleren Abschlusses voraus und bereitet auf die neuesten Prüfungen zur Erlangung der Fachhochschulreife vor. Das Lehrwerk führt zur Stufe B2 des Gemeinsamen europäischen Referenzrahmens.

Focus on Success – The new edition: Allgemeine Ausgabe ist ein komplett neu erarbeitetes Lehrwerk und bietet neue, interessante Texte, aktuelle Themen und einen auf die Lehrpläne und Prüfungen abgestimmten Aufgabenapparat. Die bewährte Struktur wurde beibehalten: Auf den *Refresher Course* folgen 12 *Main Course*-Units, die einheitlich aufgebaut sind:

> *Focus:* Der Einstieg ins Thema – bildgesteuert, anregend und motivierend.

> Text A (*Personal perspectives*) betrachtet das Thema der Unit aus einer persönlichen Perspektive.

> Text B (*The bigger picture*) behandelt die gleichen Aspekte in ihrer Wechselwirkung mit Gesellschaft, Politik und Umwelt.

> *Further options* bietet Zusatzmaterialien zur Erweiterung und individuellen Schwerpunktsetzung.

Die Übungen, die auf die Texte folgen, schulen eine Vielzahl von *Skills* und trainieren darüber hinaus alle Aufgabentypen, die in den Abschlussprüfungen vorkommen.

Die Grammatik befindet sich in **Focus on Success – The new edition: Allgemeine Ausgabe** am Ende jeder Unit in einem *Grammar checkpoint*.

Der Anhang bietet neben einer *Grammar summary* umfangreiche Wörterverzeichnisse und einen Leitfaden zu Lernstrategien.

Liebe Schülerinnen und Schüler,

Focus on Success – The new edition: Allgemeine Ausgabe ist Ihr neuer Begleiter auf dem Weg zur Fachhochschulreife. Verschaffen Sie sich einen kurzen Überblick über das Buch, und Sie werden darin alles finden, was Sie für einen erfolgreichen Englischunterricht benötigen.

Sie möchten ...

> Ihre Grundkenntnisse aufpolieren, um für die Arbeit mit längeren Texten besser gerüstet zu sein?
Kein Problem, der *Refresher Course* bringt Grammatik und Wortschatz wieder auf Vordermann – in sechs Units, jeweils anhand eines interessanten Magazinartikels.

> eine grammatische Form nachschlagen?
Dann schauen Sie einfach hinten in der *Grammar summary* oder der Liste der *Irregular verbs* nach.

> Tipps und Hilfen für den Umgang mit schwierigen Texten und kniffligen Aufgaben bekommen?
Dann werden Sie in dem Teil *Skills* im Anhang fündig – hier finden Sie zahlreiche Tipps, die Ihnen helfen, das Lernen effektiver zu gestalten.

> Vokabeln so lernen, dass Sie sie nicht gleich wieder vergessen?
In der *Unit word list* im Anhang ist der Lerneffekt gleich doppelt: Neben der deutschen Übersetzung lernen Sie auch Wörter mit gleicher oder gegensätzlicher Bedeutung, kurze und bündige Umschreibungen usw.

> Ihren Grundwortschatz wiederholen?
Die *Basic word list* bietet Ihnen alle wichtigen Wörter – thematisch geordnet, damit Sie nicht nur einzelne Wörter, sondern ganze Wortfelder auffrischen können.

Viel Spaß und Erfolg mit dem Buch!

Autoren und Redaktion

CONTENTS

Refresher Course

Main Course

Appendix

A

Free-time activities

1 TALKING ABOUT YOURSELF

How do you spend your free time? Just chilling out, or doing something more active like sport? Use the language in the speech bubbles and the ideas in the box to talk about what you do.

chilling out | clubbing | dancing | doing sport | fishing | going to LAN parties | going to the movies | hanging out with friends | listening to music | making/mixing music | playing computer/video games | playing online poker | reading | riding | sending text messages / images with a mobile | shopping | surfing the net | talking to friends on the telephone | visiting chat rooms | watching TV/DVDs

2 CARRYING OUT A SURVEY

A Ask other people what they like – or don't like – doing in their free time.

What's your favourite free-time activity?
What do you like doing most, ... or ...?
Which (activity) do you prefer, ... or ...?
Do you enjoy reading / doing a sport / ...?
Do you belong to a sports club / ...?
How much time do you spend playing computer games / ... every day/week?

B Now carry out a survey. Which are the three most popular activities in your class?

According to the media, young people today spend too much of their free time just sitting in front of televisions or computers. But is this true? We asked four young people to describe their free-time activities. Read what they had to say.

< DANA ***I spend most of my free time working for the Red Cross.*** *I really feel that I'm doing something worthwhile, not just sitting in front of the box! This week we're working with the homeless. That may not sound like fun, but I get a lot out of it. My brother Lee says I should enjoy life while I'm young, but he doesn't know what he's talking about. I'm sure that I'm having more fun than he is at the moment!*

> LUCY ***Free time? Are you joking?*** *I work three evenings a week and all day Saturday too – I don't have much time for anything else. And then there's my mum. She says I can only have a job if my schoolwork doesn't suffer. So when I get home after work I usually do my homework and go to bed. When I go out, I enjoy looking round the shops with my friends. But that doesn't happen very often, I'm afraid.*

< RAVI ***I'm playing in the first team of my football club*** *this season, so that takes up most of my free time. We train twice a week, you see, and then I usually have matches at the weekend. When I'm not playing football, I hang around with my friends or just chill out. I really like clubbing, but that's difficult in the football season. The coach expects us to keep fit and I don't want him to take me off the team.*

> SAM ***What do I do in my free time?*** *Well, I enjoy playing computer games most, I suppose, but I don't like the violent stuff. I prefer the games that test your skill against other players. I often network with other players online or go to LAN parties. They're really cool. I make a lot of new friends that way. At the moment, we're planning a big international LAN party. People are coming to it from all over the place.*

3 LOOKING AT THE TEXT

Join the beginnings (1–6) to the endings (a–f) to make sentences about the texts.

1 An international LAN party could
2 The four young people all have
3 One of the four people doesn't have
4 Dana's voluntary work with the Red Cross
5 Competitive computer games have the
6 Some parents say that part-time jobs

a can have a bad effect on schoolwork.
b makes her feel good about herself.
c much free time because she has a job.
d advantage of bringing people together.
e be a great way to make new friends.
f very different interests.

4 WORKING WITH WORDS

A Find words/expressions in the texts above to fit the definitions.

DANA
1 adjective: useful, valuable
2 people without a permanent home
3 certain

RAVI
4 noun: time of year during which something happens
5 noun: competitive game
6 verb: relax by doing nothing

LUCY
7 opposite of 'being serious'
8 verb: become worse
9 another expression for 'I'm sorry to say'

SAM
10 verb: like one thing more than another
11 noun: ability to do sth
12 verb: English for German *vernetzen*

B **Complete the sentences with six of the words/expressions from exercise A. They are not necessarily in the same order. Sometimes you must change the form.**

1 My team has an important ... today.
2 A lot of employers say social ... are as important as qualifications.
3 Can you call back later, please? ... Ms Barton is in a meeting at the moment.
4 When parents work too hard, family life always ...
5 DVDs are OK, I suppose, but I ... to see films at the cinema.
6 Can't you do something ... instead of just watching TV all the time?
7 Petrol prices always go up during the holiday ...
8 You're ...! You don't really expect me to work all weekend, do you?

C **Say who or what the circled words refer to in the texts.**

EXAMPLE > I don't want him to take me off the team. (*Ravi*)
> *'Him' refers to Ravi's football coach.*

1 ... but I get a lot out of it. (*Dana*)
2 ... he doesn't know what he's talking about. (*Dana*)
3 I usually have matches at the weekend. (*Ravi*)
4 The coach expects us to keep fit. (*Ravi*)
5 She says I can only have a job if ... (*Lucy*)
6 But that doesn't happen very often, I'm afraid. (*Lucy*)
7 They're really cool. (*Sam*)
8 At the moment, we're planning a big international LAN party. (*Sam*)

5 LOOKING AT GRAMMAR: SUBJECT AND OBJECT PRONOUNS

Subjektform	Objektform
I	me
you	you
he/she/it	him/her/it
we	us
you	you
they	them

A **Replace the underlined words with suitable subject pronouns.**

1 <u>John and Ann</u> often go cycling at the weekend.
2 Does <u>Jack</u> belong to a sports club?
3 <u>Sharon</u> spends too much time in chat rooms.
4 <u>Paul</u> scored the goal from a distance of 30 metres.

B **Now use object pronouns.**

5 A lot of people enjoy going to <u>LAN parties</u>.
6 I'm lucky. My parents pay for <u>my mobile</u>.
7 Jack phones <u>Sharon</u> five or six times a day.
8 We meet <u>Joshua</u> in town every Friday.

6 LOOKING AT GRAMMAR: SIMPLE PRESENT

Form

*Lucy and her friends **enjoy** shopping.* *Sam **plays** computer games.*	wie der Infinitiv, außer in der **3. Person Singular** *(he, she, it)*, die auf *-s* endet
*Lucy **wishes** she had more free time.* *Ravi **tries** to keep fit.* *Dana **has** more fun than her brother **does**.*	Besonderheiten der 3. Person Singular: > endet das Verb auf *-ch, -sh, -s, -x*, folgt *-es* > endet das Verb auf Konsonant + *-y*, wird die Endung zu ***-ies*** Sonderformen: *do* – ***does***, *go* – ***goes***, *have* – ***has***, *be* – ***am/are/is***
*I **do not** / **don't want** to lose my place on the first team.* *Sam **does not** / **doesn't like** violent games.*	**Verneinung:** *do not / don't* bzw. *does not / doesn't* (3. Person)
***How do** you **spend** your free time?* ***Does** Lucy **work** on Saturdays?*	**Fragen:** *do* bzw. *does*

Gebrauch

*I'm still at school and I also **have** a job.* *Sam often **goes** to LAN parties.*	für **Dauerzustände** und **wiederholte**, oft **regelmäßige Ereignisse** bzw. Handlungen

> Das **simple present** steht häufig mit den folgenden **Zeitangaben**:
- *always, often, sometimes, rarely/seldom* (selten), *never*
- *generally* (im Allgemeinen), *normally, regularly, usually* (gewöhnlich)
- *every day/week/month/..., every morning/afternoon/...*
- *on Mondays/Tuesdays/...*
- *on weekdays / during the week, at weekends / the weekend / ...*

> Kurze **Adverbien der Häufigkeit** wie *often, never* usw. stehen unmittelbar vor dem Vollverb.
*Lucy **never** goes out during the week.*

A Put the verbs into the correct form of the simple present. Be careful about negatives and questions.

1 My mate Josh ...1 (*spend*) a lot of time playing online poker, but he ...2 (*not play*) for money.

2 A ...1 (*Lucy/meet*) her friends in town every day?
B No, of course she ...2 (*not meet*) them every day. She usually ...3 (*meet*) them on Tuesdays and Fridays, I ...4 (*think*).

3 A ...1 (*you/watch*) much TV?
B Well, I ...2 (*not watch*) TV at all during the week, but I ...3 (*enjoy*) watching a good film at weekends.

4 I ...1 (*belong*) to a football club but I ...2 (not play) in the first team because I just ...3 (*not have*) the time to train twice a week.

5 A What ...1 (*Frank/do*) in his free time? ...2 (*you/know*)?
B He ...3 (*play*) the drums in a rock band and so he ...4 (*not do*) anything else really.

6 Girls ...1 (*not surf*) the net as much as boys. ...2 (*you/think*) that ...3 (*be*) the reason why girls' marks ...4 (*be*) often better than boys' marks at school?

B **Work with a partner. Use the ideas below and the activities on page 6 to tell your partner what you normally/often/sometimes/never/... do or don't do and when.**

argue with my parents/brother/sister | catch the bus | come home late | do homework | email friends | get up | go clubbing/dancing/shopping | go to school / to the cinema / to the pub / to bed | leave for school / leave the house

EXAMPLES
> I **usually go** to bed at about 11 o'clock **on weekdays**.
> My mate and I **often go** to LAN parties **at the weekend**.
> I **don't watch / never watch** TV **during the week**.

C **Now ask your partner about what he/she does or does not do. Add other activities if you wish.**

EXAMPLES
> **When** do you leave for school?
> **How often** do you work?
> **Where** do you go shopping?
> **Do** you **go** to LAN parties?

D **Report back to the class. Say what your partner does and when.**

Bernd usually goes clubbing on Saturdays.

Kathrin and her sister often play computer games.

7 LOOKING AT GRAMMAR: PRESENT PROGRESSIVE

Form	
I ***am / I'm playing*** *in the first team this season.* *At the moment, we* ***are / we're planning*** *a LAN party.*	*am/is/are* + *-ing*-Form des Vollverbs
When I ***am / I'm not working****, I'm sleeping.* *You* ***are / You're not*** *just* ***sitting*** *in front of the box.*	**Verneinung:** *not* unmittelbar nach *am/is/are*
Are you *helping homeless people, Dana?* ***Is Ravi*** *training at the moment?*	**Fragen:** Austausch von Subjekt und *am/is/are*
Gebrauch	
I ***am working*** *at a supermarket.* *We* ***are helping*** *homeless people.*	für Situationen und Ereignisse, die im Moment des Sprechens bzw. Schreibens tatsächlich im Gange sind

> Das **present progressive** steht häufig mit den folgenden **Zeitangaben**:
at present, at the moment, currently, now
> Normalerweise haben folgende Verben **keine** Verlaufsform:
be, believe, dislike, hate, know, like, love, mean, notice, see, seem, think (= meinen), *understand, want, wish*

A Put the verbs into the correct form of the present progressive.

1 The players ... (*have*) a shower at the moment.
2 Wait a minute, please. I ... (*talk*) to a customer.
3 Dana ...[1] (*not work*) with old people. She ...[2] (*help*) the homeless at present.
4 A What ...[1] (*you/do*), Sam? B I ...[2] (*try*) to organize a LAN party.
5 A Why ...[1] (*Lucy/cry*)? B She ...[2] (*not cry*). She has a cold, that's all.
6 A Can you two help me, please? B Can't it wait? We ... (*serve*) meals.
7 Jack ...[1] (*not ride*) an ordinary bike. He ...[2] (*use*) an exercise bike.
8 Lucy's mum is very angry. Lucy ... (*work*) so many hours at the moment that she doesn't have time for her schoolwork.

B Use the present progressive to ask each other questions with *what* and *who*.

EXAMPLES
> What is Tom doing/practising?
> Who is practising penalties?
> Tom is practising penalties.

cycle to the shops | do keep-fit exercises | get money from a cash machine | meet friends at the pub | play poker | practise penalties | surf the internet | take the dog for a walk | try on some shoes | wash the car

1 Tom

2 Mary + Julie

3 Brian + Sam

4 Tracey

5 Dick + Ella

6 Josh + Becky

7 Kate

8 Lee + Vera

9 Helen

10 Janna

8 MANAGING SITUATIONS

Sie möchten jemandem auf Englisch sagen, dass ...

1 ... Peter Drexler nicht mehr für Ihren Club spielt. Jetzt spielt er irgendwo in Norddeutschland, aber seinen neuen Club kennen Sie nicht.
2 ... Sie sich für Online-Poker interessieren und viel Freizeit damit verbringen.
3 ... Markus mit einem Freund gerade ein Computerprogramm schreibt.
4 ... Jasmin in der Woche meist zu Hause bleibt, da sie viel für die Schule tun muss.
5 ... Sie zurzeit Geld sparen, da Sie ein Auto kaufen wollen.
6 ... Sie einen neuen Job bei einer Pizzeria haben, Ihre Eltern aber wegen der Schule dagegen sind.
7 ... Ihr Bruder im Moment zu viel Zeit vor dem Fernseher verbringt.
8 ... die meisten Leute gar keine Freizeitbeschäftigung ausüben.

B

Girls fight for their rights

'Title IX' is a law that bans sex discrimination in US public schools[1]. One requirement of this law is that girls must have exactly the same chance to do sports as boys. The result? Girls have to join boys' teams if there are not enough girls to make up a team of their own. Read on to find out more.

Last March, Ashley Moore, 18, faced an awesome challenge[2]. She walked on to a wrestling mat to fight against her school's biggest wrestling rival. As he looked at her with hard, unblinking[3] eyes, Ashley felt a shiver of fear. Was she crazy? She was about to wrestle a hunk of a guy[4].

Four minutes later, however, Ashley walked off the mat a winner - and the hunk left on a stretcher. "He was big and strong, but he was slow," says Ashley of Edison High School, Richmond, Virginia. "He always tried the same hold. Then I took his arm and twisted it behind his back. When I did that, I pulled his back muscles. I didn't want to injure him. That's not what wrestling is about."

Ashley Moore is one of a growing number of American high school girls who play on boys' sports teams. While that can be tough, fighting stereotypes can be even tougher. But Ashley and girls like her are showing week after week that girls can compete against boys - and win.

Ashley had to fight hard to earn the respect of her male teammates. At the first training session, they greeted her with funny looks and nasty jokes. "Some of my teammates didn't say a word. They just looked at me," says Ashley. "Other boys said stuff like 'Hi sweetie, the volleyball team's next door. Aren't you at the wrong training session?'"

But Ashley didn't listen to the jokes and set to work - and soon she really impressed her teammates. "When they couldn't beat me in training," she says, "they soon backed off."

However, Ashley, who is called Xena after the TV warrior princess by her fans, doesn't want guys to back off. In fact, when she's on the mat, she wants to be their equal in every way.

1 **public school (AE) = state school (BE)** *staatliche Schule*
2 **awesome challenge** *überwältigende Herausforderung*
3 **unblinking** *unbewegt*
4 **hunk of a guy** *Kerl wie ein Baum*

1 LOOKING AT THE TEXT

Read the speech bubbles and the list of people in the box. Then decide who said each statement.

a female ice-hockey player | a first aider | Ashley | Ashley's mother | Ashley's opponent | one of Ashley's fans | one of Ashley's teammates | the wrestling coach at Edison High

1 *At first I said Ashley should do something, well, more 'feminine'. But now I'm so proud of her!*

2 *I had to take her because of Title IX. There's no girls' wrestling team at Edison High, you see.*

3 *I thought, "No problem, she's just a girl", but she taught me a lesson. I won't be able to wrestle again this season.*

4 *Ashley doesn't look like Xena, but she's our warrior princess. We never miss a match.*

5 *Ashley's hard to beat – very fast, very clever. We're all glad she's on the team now.*

6 *Ashley's right. I had problems at the beginning too, but after a couple of games the boys accepted me.*

7 *My partner said, "Let's go and get the girl off the mat." Then we realized it was the boy.*

8 *Well, I watch a lot of wrestling on TV with my dad. I thought, "Why not?"*

2 WORKING WITH WORDS

A Find words in the text and introduction that fit the definitions below.

1 verb: synonym for '(to) forbid' (ll. 1–5)
2 adjective: opposite of 'private' (ll. 1–5)
3 adverb: synonym for 'precisely' (ll. 1–5)
4 verb: synonym for '(to) put together' (ll. 1–5)
5 adjective: 'difficult or frightening' (ll. 1–5)
6 adjective: synonym for 'mad' (ll. 6–10)
7 noun: opposite of 'loser' (ll. 6–10)
8 adjective: opposite of 'weak' (ll. 11–15)
9 adjective: synonym for 'increasing' (ll. 16–20)
10 adjective: synonym for 'very difficult' (ll. 16–20)
11 noun: 'member of the same team' (ll. 21–25)
12 adjective: opposite of 'nice', 'pleasant' (ll. 26–30)

B Now write six sentences of your own about sport, using words you found in exercise 7 A.

C Copy the table and fill in the missing forms from the text.

	Verb	Noun
1	...	ban
2	(to) discriminate	...
3	(to) require	...
4	(to) challenge	...
5	(to) rival	...
6	...	wrestler
7	(to) win	...
8	...	injury
9	...	competition
10	...	impression

D Complete the sentences using words from the table on page 13. Sometimes you must change the form.

1 Many EU countries have a ... on smoking in pubs.
2 It is harder for women to play sport because there is so much ... against them.
3 Ashley took part in an important wrestling ... in Charlotteville yesterday.
4 Ashley's biggest ... has challenged her to fight him again when he's fit.
5 When she beat them in training, Ashley's skill ... her teammates.
6 A lot of people were surprised when Ashley left the mat as the ...

3 LOOKING AT GRAMMAR: SIMPLE PAST

Form

*Ashley **walked** off the mat a winner.* *I **took** his arm and twisted it behind his back.*	**regelmäßig**: Infinitiv + *-ed* **unregelmäßig**: Sonderform, s. S. 245
*Some of my teammates **didn't say** a word.*	**Verneinung**: *did not / didn't* + Infinitiv
***Did I win** just because I'm a girl?*	**Fragen**: *did* + Subjekt + Infinitiv

Gebrauch

*Ashley **faced** an awesome challenge last March.* *This big guy **backed off** at a match last week.*	für Handlungen/Situationen, die in der Vergangenheit abgeschlossen wurden

Signalwörter

yesterday, the day before yesterday	*in 1973/2007/...*
two/three/... days/weeks/months/years ago	*at that time / in those days*
last week/month/year/summer/Christmas/...	*when he/she was a child / at school / ...*
the week/month before last	

1 2 **A Complete the report with the simple past of verbs from the box. Then listen to the CD to check your answers.**

agree | give | grow up | hear | kick | live | not be | not do | not even have | not go | promise | talk

Otis Shipley ...[1] in the poorest part of Perryton, a small town in Texas. He ...[2] with his mother and four brothers and sisters. Otis didn't know his father and sometimes the family ...[3] enough money to buy food. But Otis had one thing going for him: his skill as a footballer. Nobody could run as fast as Otis and nobody ...[4] the ball as far as Otis.

It ...[5] long before Duane Tyler, the football coach at the Robert E. Lee High School in Abilene, ...[6] about Otis's phenomenal talent. Tyler went to Perryton and ...[7] to Mrs Shipley. He ...[8] her that she would have money, a nice house and a future for her children. How could she say no? Mrs Shipley soon ...[9] to move to Abilene.

And Otis didn't disappoint her. Although he ...[10] anything except play football and often ...[11] to his classes, his teachers still ...[12] him top grades.

B This is a page from Ellie Brown's weekly planner. Use the simple past to say what Ellie and her friends did last week. Add any further details if necessary.

EXAMPLES
> Ellie rang Ben and Annie about tennis at lunchtime on Monday.
> Ben and Annie had a phone call from Ellie about tennis on Monday.

MARCH		
14	Monday	lunchtime: ring Ben & Annie (tennis) evening: do ironing!!
15	Tuesday	8:00 a.m. take bike to Apex Bikes 3:15 p.m. hairdresser's ✕ on way home: bank, pay garage bill
16	Wednesday	late afternoon: pick up bike (Apex)
17	Thursday	5:30 p.m. meet Mandy, Annie (Virgin Media) buy birthday present (Sam)
18	Friday	6–8 p.m. training, swimming competition 9:30 p.m.–11:00 p.m. record film, BBC2
19	Saturday	10 a.m. meet Mandy (power walking, Mousehold Heath)
20	Sunday	visit Kate (hospital, Ward 4) GET BOOK – NO FRUIT, NO FLOWERS!!

C Work with a partner. Use the words in the box and the simple past to ask your partner what he or she did *yesterday / last night / last weekend / last summer / last Christmas / …*. Swap roles at least once.

go riding/camping/dancing/swimming/shopping/… | go to a disco / the gym / the leisure centre / the movies / a party / the pub / … | go on holiday / a trip / a cycle tour to … | have a date | meet sb | play basketball/cards / computer games / football / …

EXAMPLES
> Did you go to the pub last Friday?
> Yes, I did. / No, I didn't. I went to a party at Paula's.

> What did you do last weekend?
> We went shopping on Saturday, but I stayed at home on Sunday.

4 MANAGING SITUATIONS

Sie möchten jemandem auf Englisch sagen, dass …

1 … Ihr Fußballverein gestern den Pokal gegen eine holländische Mannschaft gewonnen hat.
2 … es Donnerstag Abend kein Training gab, da der Trainer krank war.
3 … Sie und Ihr Bruder am Sonntag eine 60-km-Radtour gemacht haben.
4 … Sie vor zwei Monaten Golf ausprobiert haben, aber das Spiel äußerst langweilig fanden.
5 … Sie und Ihre Familie letztes Jahr einen Campingurlaub in Italien gemacht haben.
6 … Ihr Kanuverein letzten Samstag eine tolle Saisonabschlussfeier (*end-of-season party*) hatte.

You are what you eat

BEFORE YOU READ

What do you think the text might be about?

A case study: **Maddy Johnson's double life**

A lot of people eat too much food or spend too much time sitting in front of the TV. That's OK because if they eat less and do more exercise, they can become healthy.
But some people have a genuine problem. They have an eating disorder like anorexia[1] or bulimia[2]. Read on to find out more ...

Maddy Johnson is charming, attractive and successful. She's popular, too – at school, in her part-time job and in her community. Everybody loves Maddy. But the reality is different. Maddy is leading a double life – the public one and a secret one that nobody sees. Maddy is ill. She suffers from bulimia.

The poster outside the fast-food restaurant showed a double-decker cheeseburger with an XXL packet of fries, two little tubs of sauce and a big can of coke. "Today's Special!" it screamed. "Buy two cheeseburgers and get free fries!"

Maddy looked at the poster and had that familiar, tingling feeling. It was like sex. "No!" she said to herself. "Just walk away! You don't want it! You don't need it!" But that was the problem, wasn't it? Maddy couldn't 'just walk away'. It was as if she had lost control over her own body.

Maddy went into the restaurant and bought two cheeseburgers with free fries. She walked to an empty table and sat down with her back to the room. She didn't want people to see how she stuffed the burgers greedily into her mouth. In no time, she was back at the counter. She ordered a dessert: an XL tub of ice cream with caramel sauce and two cream donuts. The guy behind the counter looked at her. "Hungry, are we?" he said with a cheeky grin. "He knows," thought Maddy. She wanted to sink through the floor.

Maddy finished her meal and went into the toilets. The tingling had stopped, but she hated herself. She felt dirty and so guilty. She went into a cubicle, bent over the toilet pan and threw up.

When she came out of the cubicle, a woman was washing her hands. "Are you all right?" she asked. "That sounded ... Well, I couldn't help hearing. I'm so sorry." The woman offered Maddy a card. 'Ellen Anderson, National Association for Eating Disorders', it said. It gave the number of a free hotline and Ellen's email address. "Will you let me help you?" Ellen asked. Maddy looked at her. "It's OK," she said. "What do you mean 'help me'? I'm fine. Really. I just felt sick, that's all. I don't need ... Well, I mean, ..." "You don't have to explain, dear. I've been down that road as well. I *know*. You just can't beat this illness alone. Please ring that number, day or night."

1 anorexia: refusal to eat for fear of putting on weight *Magersucht*
2 bulimia: addiction to food and vomiting to lose weight *Ess-Brech-Sucht*

1 LOOKING AT THE TEXT

A Do the following tasks.

1 Compare Maddy's public and secret lives.
2 Describe how Maddy felt a) outside the restaurant and b) when she went into the toilets.
3 Find evidence to show that Maddy felt embarrassed and ashamed of herself in the restaurant.
4 Describe Maddy's reaction to Ellen Anderson's offer of help. What does it tell us about Maddy's attitude to her illness?
5 Explain how we know that Ellen Anderson really understood Maddy's problem.

B Read the speech bubbles and say which opinion about eating disorders you agree or disagree with most. Give reasons for your choice.

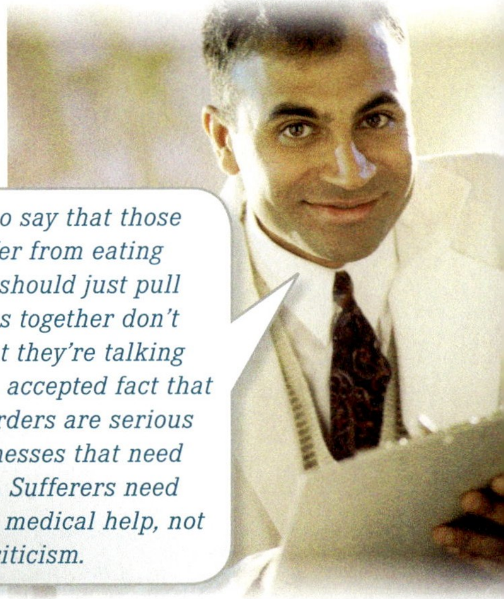

2 WORKING WITH WORDS

A Read the introduction and the case study again. Complete the table with the missing verbs.

verb + noun / noun phrase			
(to) eat	*too much food*	*(to) ...*	*food into one's mouth*
(to) ...	*an eating disorder*	*(to) ...*	*a dessert*
(to) ...	*bulimia*	*(to) ...*	*a meal*
(to) ...	*a cheeseburger*	*(to) ...*	*an illness*
(to) ...	*free fries*		

B Complete the sentences with verbs from exercise A. Make sure the verb is in the right form.

1 I'm sure Alice can ... bulimia if she gets help from a doctor.
2 I always ... too much chocolate at Easter.
3 Two years ago Sally was very thin because she ... anorexia.
4 At this restaurant you ... a free dessert with every meal.
5 George must be hungry – he is ... that cake into his mouth!
6 I ... chicken but the waiter brought me fish.

C Replace the underlined words with a synonym from the text. They are in the same order.

1 Many burger bars attract customers with special offers. *A lot of*
2 People who drink too much alcohol get drunk.
3 Do you have a real reason for not any doing exercise today?
4 The difficulty is that "natural food" is too expensive for most people.
5 Everybody knows that good-looking people have an easier life.
6 I live in a mixed neighbourhood with people from all over the place.
7 The truth of most people's lives is far from what you see in TV ads.
8 The driver of the car was so angry that she shouted at me.
9 The film was really disgusting. Afterwards I was sick.
10 It is almost impossible to overcome an eating disorder without help.

3 WRITING

Imagine you are Maddy. Use your answers from exercise 1 A to write an email to Ellen Anderson asking for her help.

Email

Hi Ellen

Thanks for giving me your email address. I think you are right – yes, I have a problem and I just don't know what to do about it. I feel so ...

4 LOOKING AT GRAMMAR: POSSESSIVE ADJECTIVES

> **Possessive adjectives** zeigen an, wem irgendetwas gehört. Sie stehen – wie andere Adjektive – unmittelbar vor dem Nomen.

I	*Maddy is **my** sister.*	
you	*Can you tell me **your** name, please?*	
he	*What is **his** job?*	
she	*Is Joshua **her** brother?*	
it	*Wales is in the UK. **Its** capital is Cardiff.*	⚠ **it's** = it is
we	*There are 1,500 students at **our** school.*	
you	*Please open **your** books at page 23.*	
they	***Their** home is in London.*	⚠ **there** = *da, dort*

Complete these sentences with the English equivalent of the words in brackets.

1 What's *your name* (*dein Name*), please?
2 He's walking home because ... (*sein Rad*) is broken.
3 Maddy is writing ... (*ihrer Freundin*) an email.
4 Unfortunately the students have to buy ... (*ihre Bücher*) themselves.
5 The trainer asked me for ... (*meinem Gewicht*).
6 This table is too small for ... (*unsere Gruppe*).
7 The doctor thinks ... (*ihre Krankheit*) is curable.
8 You shouldn't give ... (*Ihren Kindern*) so much fatty food.
9 (*Ihr Name*) ... is Madison, but she calls herself 'Maddy'.
10 Look at that poor bird. What's the matter with ... (*seinem Bein*)?

5 LOOKING AT GRAMMAR: COUNTABLE AND UNCOUNTABLE NOUNS

Maddy ordered **a dessert**. *She had* **an ice cream** *and* **two donuts**.	*dessert, ice cream, donuts* usw. = **zählbare Nomen** (Pluralform möglich, können mit Zahlwörtern oder *a/an* verwendet werden)
I'd like **cheese** *and* **mayonnaise** *on my burger, please.*	*cheese, mayonnaise* usw. = **nicht zählbare Nomen** (keine Pluralform, keine Verwendung mit Zahlwörtern oder *a/an*)
Oliver had **two cups of tea, a plate of ham and eggs** *and* **a bowl of corn pops** *for breakfast.*	bei nicht zählbaren Nomen: Pluralbildung durch Hinzufügen eines **zählbaren Nomens** wie *two cups of …, a plate of …, a bowl of …*
Research *shows that bulimia is a serious illness. Ellen gave Maddy* **some advice** *about bulimia. Two recent* **pieces of news** *showed that exercise is very important.*	**nicht zählbare Sammelbegriffe**: *luggage, furniture, hardware/software* sowie *advice, evidence, information, knowledge, news* und *research* stehen mit Verben im Singular; **Pluralbildung** mit *pieces of …* (formell) bzw. *bits of …* (weniger formell)

⚠ **Beachten Sie**, dass wir die Nomen *people* und *police* nur im Plural verwenden können. Wollen wir sie im **Singular** gebrauchen, benutzen wir ***person*** für *people* und ***police officer*** für *police*.

> *The* **people** *in the café* **were** *drinking coffee. Only* **one person was** *drinking wine.*
> **A police officer** *said that* **the police were** *on their way.*

A In your exercise book, draw a table for countable and uncountable nouns like the one below. Put the nouns in box A into the correct column.

B Give the plural form of the countable nouns. Add a suitable countable expression from box B to the uncountables so that you can use them in the plural.

A

box | bread | bus | car | cheese | child | chocolate | coffee | evidence | family | fish | glass | house | kiss | knife | meat | mustard | news | oil | paint | people | water | woman | yoghurt

B

bars/pieces of | bits/pieces of | bottles/glasses of | cans/tins of | crowds/queues of | cups of | loaves/slices of | pairs of | slices of | tubs of | tubes/sticks of

Countable		Uncountable	
Singular	Plural	Base form	Qualified form
box	*boxes*	*bread*	*loaves/slices of bread*

C Now write five sentences using some of the expressions from exercise B. Be careful with singular/plural verbs.

6 LOOKING AT GRAMMAR: UNSPECIFIED QUANTITIES

> *Some, any* und ihre Zusammensetzungen

*Please add **some** salt to the potatoes.*	**bejahte Aussagen:** *some*
*We don't have **any** butter. Use olive oil.* *Did you put **any** salt on the potatoes?*	**verneinte Aussagen** und **Fragen:** *any*
*May I have **some** salt, please?* *Can I get you **some** orange juice, Maddy?*	**Bitten** und **Angebote**, die wahrscheinlich mit **ja** beantwortet werden: *some*
*There is **something** wrong with the toaster.* *I didn't see **anybody** I know at the pub.* *Have you seen the cookbook **anywhere**?*	**Zusammensetzungen** von *some/any* werden genauso verwendet

A Complete the sentences with *some* or *any*.

1 Do you have *any* mustard, please?
2 We don't need ... bread.
3 There is ... butter in the kitchen.
4 It was awful. ... men had too much to drink and started a fight.
5 Would you like ...[1] more fries? You can have ...[2] of mine. I don't want ...[3] more.
6 The party was a bit boring because there wasn't ... music.
7 Don't forget to buy ...[1] drinking chocolate or we won't have ...[2] for breakfast.
8 We can't invite ...[1] more people to the party. We don't have ...[2] room.

B Complete the sentences with *somebody/anybody*, *something/anything* or *somewhere/anywhere*.

1 A Listen! I think there's *somebody*[1] at the door.
B I didn't hear *anything*[2]. I don't think there's ...[3] there.
2 I can't find the shopping list. Have you seen it ...[1]? It must be here ...[2].
3 A Did you buy ...[1] to drink?
B Well, I bought some mineral water, but I expect you'd like ...[2] stronger.
4 I need ...[1] to help with the barbecue on Saturday. Can you think of ...[2] we could ask?
5 We need some more coke. If you're not doing ..., could you go and buy some?
6 Do you know ... who can mix cocktails, Janna?

> *Much, many, a lot of* und *plenty of*

*We don't need **many steaks**.* *How **many tomatoes** do we need?* *I don't use **much salt** in my cooking.* *How **much butter** do we have?*	**verneinte Aussagen und Fragen:** *many* mit **zählbaren** und *much* mit **nicht zählbaren** Nomen
***A lot of/Lots of children** are too fat.* *Maddy eats **a lot of food** and then she makes herself sick.*	**bejahte Aussagen:** *a lot of* oder *lots of* (weniger formell) bei **zählbaren** und **nicht zählbaren Nomen**
*Drink **as much water** as you like.* *We bought far **too many steaks**.*	**Beachten Sie:** *much/many* nach *as, how, so, too* und *very* auch in **bejahten Aussagen**
*There's **plenty of bread** in the freezer.*	„viel" in der Bedeutung „mehr als genug": *plenty of* statt *a lot of / lots of*

C **Complete the sentences with *much, many, a lot of* or *plenty of*.**

1 There weren't *many*[1] people at the supermarket. I think *a lot of*[2] people are away on holiday at the moment.

2 A Hurry up! We don't have ...[1] time.
B Don't panic. We have ...[2] time. The shops don't close until 10 o'clock.
A Really? I thought they closed ...[3] earlier than that.

3 A How ...[1] people are coming to the barbecue on Saturday?
B Not ...[2]. Six, I think.
A Only six? Why on earth did you buy so ...[3] meat then?

4 You needn't go shopping. We have ...[1] food in the freezer and we won't need ...[2] drink. ...[3] people are driving.

5 ...[1] women work at supermarkets but not ...[2] of them have a top job.

6 A John eats ...[1] chocolate, doesn't he?
B Yes. He eats far too ...[2] sweets and he shouldn't drink so ...[3] coke, either.

> ***(A) little, (a) few***

*Add **a little water** if necessary.* (ein wenig) *Jake has **little interest** in food.* (nur wenig)	**nicht zählbare Nomen:** *(a) little*
*You need **a few carrots**, too.* (ein paar) ***Few cooks** are as good as she is.* (nur wenig)	**zählbare Nomen:** *(a) few*

D **Complete the sentences with *(a) little* or *(a) few*.**

1 A Can I give you *a few*[1] more fries?
B No, thanks, but I'd like *a little*[2] more bread, please.

2 A Why did you buy so much beer?
B Because we only have ... cans in the fridge.

3 A Nobody gets fat at Brenda's parties. You only get ...[1] bread.
B Be fair. Last time we got ...[2] bits of cheese, too.

4 A Most doctors say that you should only use ...[1] salt.
B Sure, but only ...[2] doctors follow their own advice.

5 A There's ...[1] point in saying anything. The boss never listens to us.
B I know, but I have ...[2] questions I want to ask him.

6 A Shops can open on Sundays in the UK but only ...[1] do so.
B That's understandable. People want ...[2] time off.

7 MANAGING SITUATIONS

Sie möchten jemandem auf Englisch sagen, dass ...

1 ... Sie eine gute Nachricht haben. Die Polizei hat das Kind gefunden.
2 ... Sie nur wenig Zeit haben, da Sie noch viel Arbeit zu erledigen haben.
3 ... die medizinischen Beweise eindeutig (*conclusive*) sind. Essstörungen sind eine psychische Erkrankung. Viele junge Mädchen leiden unter Essstörungen.
4 ... Sie auf der Party viel Fisch und Käse aber nur wenig Fleisch anbieten wollen.
5 ... viel zu viele Leute Fast Food essen, weil sie keine Zeit haben, etwas gesundes zu kochen.
6 ... es dieses Jahr so viel Obst gibt, dass die Bauern nur wenig Geld verdienen. Viele lassen das Obst an den Bäumen.

D

Time out

Many young people now choose to spend some time abroad after they leave school. Holly Morris wants to do exactly that – but she can't decide where to go. So she writes an email to a magazine, asking for help with her problem.

Hi Jala
I hope other readers will help me with my problem. It's like this: I'm leaving school next July and then I'm taking time out, six months or so, to spend time abroad. I'd really like to go somewhere like Brazil or maybe India that I won't have a chance to see again. But my parents, who are going to help me financially, are totally against these 'exotic destinations'. They want me to go to a rich English-speaking country like Australia or Canada.
As I am going to work some of the time, they say it'll be easier for me to find a 'proper job' there and 'people are more like us'. But what's the point in going somewhere like that? I want to see new places and meet new people. But what can I do? My dad says that there's no way that he's going to pay for me to get myself killed!
Do you or your readers have any bright ideas?
Holly Morris

OK, Holly, so you're going to pay for some of your time out as you go – but how? Are you going to pick fruit or work in a bar, for example? If so, your dad's absolutely right. You can forget places like South America and India – and safety really is a problem, especially for girls. Please believe this, Holly, or I can see that you're going to have a lot of very nasty surprises.

1 LISTENING

1 3 **Work with a partner. Complete the email with suitable words. Then listen to the CD to check your answers.**

Hi
Look, this may sound totally uncool, Holly, but I *agree* [1] with your dad. You will find it very ... [2] to find a job in a country like Brazil, where millions of people are out of ... [3]. And even if you do find one, what are you going to do about language difficulties? Or do you ... [4] Portuguese? Come on! Let's get real!
Here's my advice. Go to a richer, English-speaking ... [5] like the USA or Australia, where you speak the ... [6] and will be able to find a job. Please remember that you won't just want to earn enough for your ordinary living expenses, either. You'll also want to save some ... [7] to travel around while you're there. Otherwise, what's the ... [8] in going?
Now, here's a tip. You will find it very difficult to organize a trip like this yourself. You need expert ... [9]. As a first step, why not visit a ... [10] like bunac.org and ... [11] the country you want to go to, Work America, for example? There you will find all the information, advice and job offers you need.
Good ... [12], Holly, and have a lot of fun!
Casey

2 LOOKING AT THE TEXT

A Draw a grid like the one below in your exercise book. Then complete it with information from the emails.

Holly	Holly's parents	Jala + Casey
– is leaving school in July	*– are going to help financially*	*– agree with Holly's parents*

B Holly is telling a friend about her plans. Use information from your grid to complete the conversation.

3 WORKING WITH WORDS

Complete the sentences with words from the emails. They are not necessarily in the same order.

1 So many tourists go to 'exotic ...' that they are no longer exotic.
2 You won't have any language ... because everyone in Australia speaks English.
3 The USA is the biggest English-speaking ... in the world.
4 My dad wants me to get a '... job', but how? I'm only here for a month or so.
5 Spending time ... can be a great way to find out about life in another country.
6 We had a nasty ... when we got home. Somebody had broken into the house.
7 You can pick ..., but you will not earn very much money.
8 Holly will have to work some of the time to pay her living ...
9 How can she find a job in Canada? Do you have any ... ideas?
10 If you've never worked in Brazil before, you should get expert ... before you leave.

4 LOOKING AT GRAMMAR: FUTURE

> Das *will future*

Form

*You **will be able to** find a job in the USA.*	*will* + Infinitiv für alle Personen
*I **will not / won't have** a chance to go there again.*	**Verneinung:** *not* unmittelbar nach *will* ⚠ Kurzform: *won't*
***Will Holly** be safer in the USA?*	**Fragen:** Austausch von Subjekt und *will*

Gebrauch

*I think you **will have** problems finding a job.* *I **won't have** a chance to go there again.* *I hope Holly **will follow** Jala's advice.*	Vorhersagen/Vermutungen/Hoffnungen über die Zukunft
*I've missed my bus. – Don't worry. I**'ll give** you a lift.*	spontane Entscheidungen
***Will** you **help** me complete this form, please?*	Bitten

> Das *going to future*

Form

*My parents **are going to help** me.*	*am/is/are going to* + Infinitiv
*We **are/'re not going to help** you get yourself killed!*	**Verneinung:** *not* unmittelbar nach *am/is/are*
***Are you** going to work in a bar, for example?*	**Fragen:** Austausch von Subjekt und *am/is/are*

Gebrauch

*Holly **is going to take** time out in the USA.*	Absichten und Pläne
*I can see that you **are going to have** a lot of nasty surprises.*	unmittelbar bevorstehende Ereignisse, für die es schon Anzeichen gibt

A Use the correct form of the *will* or *going to* future.

1 I'm sure Holly *will enjoy* (*enjoy*) her time out in Georgia.
2 Holly's parents ... (*visit*) her in the USA.
3 The weatherman on TV thinks it ... (*rain*) tomorrow.
4 Watch out! Can't you see that child ... (*run*) across the road?
5 Is it true? ... (*Casey/help*) Holly find a job?
6 We ... (*do*) our best, but I don't think your visa ... (*be*) ready by Friday.
7 Let me know what flight you're on and I ... (*meet*) you at the airport, OK?
8 Hey, Dad, ... (*you/help*) me with my luggage, please?

> Das ***present progressive*** und ***simple present*** mit zukünftiger Bedeutung

*I **am leaving** school **next July**.* *Holly **is flying** to Atlanta **at 7:30 this evening**.*	für Termine und fest geplante Vorhaben, mit Zeitangabe
*Holly's plane **takes off** at 10:30 tomorrow.* *The film **starts** at 8 o'clock on Sundays.*	für Flugpläne, Fahrpläne usw. für Kinoprogramme usw.

B Make sentences with the *going to* future or the present progressive. Only use the present progressive when there is an adverb of future time. Add any missing words.

EXAMPLES
> several school-leavers / take time out / Australia
> *Several school-leavers **are going to take** time out in Australia.*

> I / fly / Cologne next Saturday
> *I **am flying** to Cologne next Saturday.*

1 we + meet / 7 or 7:30 tomorrow?
2 we / get a job / pay for our holiday
3 you + come / Holly's farewell party / Friday?
4 Casey + work / the USA?
5 I / start work / six / and I / finish / two next week
6 A What are your plans for the summer?
B we / look for / a job on a farm in France
7 they + sell / their car / internet?
8 we / not have / holiday / next summer // we / stay at home

C Put the verbs into the correct form: *will* future, *going to* future, present progressive or simple present.

1 A What time ...[1] (*you/go*) into town tomorrow, Ann?
B Well, I ...[2] (*meet*) Ellie in the pub at 7. Jack and Sarah ...[3] (*come*), too. Why don't you come? I'm sure they ...[4] (*be*) really pleased to see you again.
A Great. I ...[5] (*definitely* + *be*) there. It ...[6] (*be*) nice to see Jack and Sarah again.

2 A Is it true that Holly ...[1] (*not come*) back home at the end of her time out?
B Who told you that? She ...[2] (*come*) home in August and then she ...[3] (*start*) college in October.

3 A The TV programme ...[1] (*start*) at 8:15 so I want to get the bus that ...[2] (*leave*) at 7:50.
B But that bus ...[3] (*not get to*) Oak Street until about 8:10. We ...[4] (*only* + *have*) five minutes to walk home. Let's take the bus that ...[5] (*go*) at 7:30, shall we?

4 A We ...[1] (*not go*) away on holiday at all next summer. We ...[2] (*spend*) the whole time at home.
B Good idea. They say we ...[3] (*have*) a very hot summer. I'm sure you ...[4] (*be*) much more comfortable at home.
A True – and we ...[5] (*save*) a lot of money, too!

5 MANAGING SITUATIONS

Sie möchten jemandem auf Englisch sagen, dass ...

1 ... es morgen sonnig sein soll.
2 ... Ihre Schwester am 10. Juli in die USA fliegt, um ihren Job in New Orleans anzufangen.
3 ... Ihre Eltern Sie während Ihrer Zeit im Ausland finanziell unterstützen werden.
4 ... Sie wissen wollen, ob Tom vorhat, eine neue Stelle zu suchen.
5 ... Mary bestimmt ein Jahr in Australien verbringen wird.
6 ... Sie am Donnerstag nicht zu Hause sind, da Sie am Mittwoch in den Urlaub nach Italien fliegen.

Shopping

Shopping online certainly has its advantages: no parking problems, no queues, no pushy sales staff, no carrying shopping home. And credit cards make it so easy to pay – too easy, perhaps. Read on to find out what that can mean.

Sharon Miller's virtual world of online shopping

Clothes and fashion are important to me. When I was a child, my mum had mail-order catalogues. I liked to look at them and make long lists of the clothes I wanted. Of course, my mum didn't buy them. She couldn't. She didn't have the money.

When I got older, I started buying my own clothes. I spent happy hours at the bargain counters of big department stores in Manchester. Then, when I was 16, I discovered a 'nearly-new' shop in King Street. My first purchase there was a fabulous blouse in the latest fashion colours for just £30.

After that, I went there every week. The clothes were cheaper than in ordinary shops and often much better quality. You see, a lot of rich, fashion-conscious women sometimes wear really expensive clothes only once. And I wanted to be like those women. I wanted the coolest and smartest and most fashionable clothes, you know, exclusive Italian designer labels like Versace, Armani and Gucci – and I wanted my wardrobe to be full of them.

When I was 18, I discovered the thrill of eBay. I always thought eBay was just for techno freaks, but how wrong I was! Once I bought a lovely Armani cocktail dress in pure silk for just £4.99!

Soon I was doing all my shopping online – not just on eBay, but at top designer sites as well. But I spent more money than I had – much, much more money. With a credit card, it was so easy. I just clicked the mouse – click, click, click into the virtual shopping trolley. But in the meantime I've run up debts of over £4,500. And they aren't virtual, they're real.

1 LOOKING AT THE TEXT

Choose the right answer to complete the statements.

1 Sharon discovered her interest in clothes by ...
 a visiting exclusive boutiques.
 b looking through mail-order catalogues.
 c searching for special offers.

2 At first, Sharon bought her clothes at ...
 a bargain counters in big stores.
 b second-hand shops.
 c exclusive designer boutiques.

3 When she was 16, Sharon ...
 a found a nearly-new shop in Manchester.
 b heard about bargains on eBay.
 c bought fashionable clothes from rich women.

4 Sharon wanted to be like ...
 a her friends who wore the latest fashions.
 b smart women who wore expensive clothes just once.
 c the other customers at the nearly-new shop.

5 Sharon thought that eBay was ...
 a only for techno freaks.
 b an internet auction site that sold everything.
 c an online clothes shop.

6 On eBay, Sharon once bought a ...
 a blouse in the latest fashion colours.
 b silk cocktail dress.
 c wardrobe full of designer clothes.

7 Soon Sharon was doing all her clothes shopping ...
 a in online shops and on eBay.
 b on eBay.
 c in ordinary shops.

8 Sharon got into debt because she ...
 a used a credit card.
 b spent much more money than she had.
 c did a lot of online shopping.

2 WORKING WITH WORDS

A Link the nouns in the box on the left with a noun from the box on the right to form compounds.

1 bargain	5 designer	9 shopping
2 cocktail	6 fashion	10 techno
3 credit	7 mail-order	
4 department	8 sales	

card | catalogue | colour | counter | dress | freak | label | staff | store | trolley

B Complete the sentences with the English equivalent of the German words or phrases in brackets. Be careful to use the correct form.

1 There are many ...[1] (*Vorteil*) in shopping online. ...[2] (*Inzwischen*) more and more people have ...[3] (*entdecken*) how easy shopping from home is.
2 Many people prefer to order goods from a ...[1] (*Versandhauskatalog*) because they don't like ...[2] (*aufdringlich*) sales assistants.
3 ...[1] (*modebewusst*) women don't like to wear the same ...[2] (*Kleidungsstück*) too often.
4 It's a crime to ... (*Schulden zusammenkommen lassen*) that you know you won't be able to pay.
5 I didn't ...[1] (*ausgeben*) much at the supermarket yesterday. In fact, I didn't even use a ...[2] (*Einkaufswagen*) as I only needed two things.
6 Clothes at the new boutique are not as ...[1] (*teuer*) as at the ...[2] (*Warenhaus*) nearby.

C First read the five golden rules. Then complete them with words from the box.

The Five Golden Rules

1 Know how much ...[1] you have. Be ...[2] and **never** just 'hope for the best'.
2 Buying for ...[1] is **always** much, much cheaper than buying ...[2].
3 Be very sceptical about ...[1]. In the end, nothing is ...[2].
4 If you ignore ...[1], it doesn't go away. It just gets worse - and ...[2].
5 Keep in touch with your ...[1]. Describe your problem honestly and say how you plan to ...[2] the debt.

cash | creditors | debt | free | free offers | money | on credit | realistic | repay | worse

3 LOOKING AT GRAMMAR: ADJECTIVES AND ADVERBS

*Sharon spent **happy** hours in boutiques.* *Shopping online is **quick** and **convenient**.*	**Adjektive** beschreiben **Nomen** Stellung: entweder unmittelbar vor dem Nomen oder nach einer Form von *be/become*
*Think about your needs **honestly**.* *All the clothes in this shop are **nearly** new.*	**Adverbien** beschreiben **Verben** oder **Adjektive**
*Sharon ran up debts **quickly**.*	Form: weitaus die meisten Adverbien enden auf *-ly*
*We must do two things **fast**.*	wichtige **unregelmäßige** Adverbien: *good* – ***well***, *fast* – ***fast***, *hard* – ***hard***
*Sharon **looks awful** in that dress.*	*(to) feel, (to) look, (to) sound, (to) taste* stehen mit **Adjektiven**

Choose the correct form of the underlined words to complete this text.

The man walked into the phone shop and went over to the display of mobile phones. He walked slow/slowly [1] along the rows of elegant/elegantly [2] phones, stopping occasional/occasionally [3] to look at a phone more close/closely [4]. But he couldn't look at them proper/properly [5]. They were all fixed firm/firmly [6] in anti-theft pads with little red lights that glowed bright/brightly [7].

An assistant came over. "Can I help you at all?" she asked polite/politely [8]. "Sure," said the man. "I need a new phone. This one looks good/well [9]." "The 6131? Well, you can't go wrong there. It's a very reliable/reliably [10] model." "Yes, but it's not cheap/cheaply [11], is it?" "You're right there," said the assistant. She smiled pleasant/pleasantly [12] at the customer. "But it's fantastic/fantastically [13] good value for money, you know. It's got every possible/possibly [14] modern feature. Let me show you." The assistant switched off the alarm and removed the phone careful/carefully [15] from its pad. "This way, please, sir," she said.

4 LOOKING AT GRAMMAR: POSITION OF ADVERBS

Satzadverbien	
Of course, *Mum didn't buy the clothes.*	**Satzanfang:** *(un)fortunately, actually, in fact, (un)luckily, maybe, perhaps, naturally, obviously*
Art und Weise	
Think about your needs ***honestly.***	**Satzende**
Ort und Zeit	
The shop is ***in King Street.*** *Mum comes home* ***at 6 o'clock.*** *The train leaves* ***Manchester at 10:30.*** *Ashley was* ***great in the match last night.***	**Satzende** Reihenfolge bei mehreren Adverbien: Ort – Zeit Art und Weise – Ort – Zeit
Häufigkeit	
We ***often*** *go shopping in King Street.* *Sharon is* ***sometimes*** *irresponsible.* *We go shopping* ***every Saturday.*** *We only go shopping* ***once a week.***	**Satzmitte:** unbestimmte Häufigkeit – vor Vollverben, nach *be* **Satzende:** bestimmte Häufigkeit sowie zusammengesetzte Häufigkeitsangaben wie *from time to time, (every) now and then*

A Say where you would put the adverbs of frequency: position A or B?

1 Retailers A say B that shoplifting is getting worse. (*often*)
2 Tough punishment A stops a shoplifter B. (*seldom*)
3 Modern technology is A catching more and more shoplifters B. (*every year*)
4 Some shoplifters are so clever that they A get caught B. (*never*)
5 Other shoppers A see people shoplifting B. (*now and then*)
6 But they don't A do B anything about it. (*usually*)

B Rewrite the sentences with the adverbs in the correct position.

1 The coat was in the sale. (*luckily*)
2 Before buying on credit, you should think about your financial situation. (*realistically*)
3 Fashionable women wear expensive clothes only once. (*sometimes*)
4 I am very tired after doing the shopping. (*always*)
5 Sharon visits the eBay site. (*several times a week*)
6 I didn't buy anything because the shop assistant spoke to me. (*rudely*)
7 The Brad Pitt film is on TV this evening. (*at 9:30, on Channel 4*)
8 I think you acted very well – congratulations! (*in the play, last night*)

5 MANAGING SITUATIONS

Sie möchten jemandem auf Englisch sagen, dass ...

1 ... nächste Woche ein neues Kaufhaus in der Stadt eröffnet.
2 ... viele Produkte online billiger sind.
3 ... man leicht Schulden macht, wenn man immer online kauft.
4 ... riesige Supermärkte viele kleinere Geschäfte ruinieren (*ruin*).
5 ... Sie versuchen so oft wie möglich in kleineren Geschäften einzukaufen.
6 ... Stadtzentren in der Zukunft ganz anders aussehen werden.

Ready for a job?

Have you ever thought of working in your spare time? If so, this questionnaire will help you to find out if you're ready to take on a part-time job as well as school.

1 DOING A QUESTIONNAIRE

Do the questionnaire by choosing the answer for each question that fits you best. Use the table opposite to work out your score and then read what your score means.

1 ***Why do you want a part-time job?***

A I've just seen a really cool new MP3 player and I have to buy it!
B I want to earn some money so I don't have to keep asking my parents to buy stuff for me.
C To get some work experience – I think it will help me find a good job when I leave college.

2 ***How much time do you spend doing your homework?***

A Some nights I stay up late working, some nights I watch TV instead.
B I usually spend an hour every evening working. That way I get all my work done and have time for other things.
C Sometimes I get home from school and start watching a DVD or texting my friends and forget all about my homework.

3 ***How often do you do out-of-school activities?***

A I do loads of stuff after school – I'm always busy!
B I'm quite lazy. When I get home from school, I just want to sit and watch TV.
C I go to one or two after-school clubs but I'm free most evenings.

4 ***How much time do you plan to spend doing your part-time job?***

A My schoolwork and my social life are important, so maybe 15 hours a week.
B As much as I can! Just think of all the money ...
C That depends on what job I get.

5 ***Are you ever late for school?***

A I always get to school on time – with my homework ready to be handed in.
B If my mum didn't wake me up every morning, I'd probably never get out of bed.
C I've missed the bus a couple of times, but I usually get to school on time.

6 ***How well do you work with other people?***

A I hate being told what to do.
B I work quite well in a group. But sometimes I just sit back and let the others do the work.
C I like meeting new people and I'm always happy to help someone out.

Scoring

Question	Answer	Points
1	A	2
	B	4
	C	6
2	A	4
	B	6
	C	2

Question	Answer	Points
3	A	2
	B	4
	C	6
4	A	6
	B	2
	C	4

Question	Answer	Points
5	A	6
	B	2
	C	4
6	A	2
	B	4
	C	6

What your score means

29–36 Congratulations! You are organized, motivated and have a really positive attitude to work – all things that employers think are really important! Getting a part-time job should be no problem for you.

21–28 You seem to be ready for a part-time job. Just make sure you don't do too much – leave enough time for doing your schoolwork and having fun.

12–20 You're not ready for a part-time job yet. You should learn to organize your time better. Forget about looking for a job and concentrate on getting your schoolwork done on time! You need to be more sensible with money too.

2 LISTENING

1 4 **Reporter Clare Harris is interviewing careers adviser Bob Jackson. Work with a partner. Read the interview and try to fill the gaps with suitable words. The words are all linked to the theme of school and work. Then listen to the CD to check your answers.**

CLARE Good morning, Bob, and thanks for seeing me.

BOB Don't mention it.

CLARE Over the last few years, more and more teenagers have taken a part-time ...¹ while they're still at school. But is that a good thing? Shouldn't they concentrate on their ...²?

BOB Well, Clare, that depends on the person. Some people do part-time work and do well at ...³ too. But others find schoolwork more difficult and might need more time for it.

CLARE But some people don't have a choice, do they? Lots of young people say they have to work just to get by – they have to earn ...⁴ to buy the things they need.

BOB I'm not sure that's true, Clare. What do they need the money for? For food or for a new mobile phone? But you're right, part-time ...⁵ among the over-16s has increased a lot since the 1990s and, in most cases, I think that's a good thing.

CLARE Really? But don't young people nowadays have much more stress in their lives because they have jobs?

BOB No, not really. People have been working their way through school for generations. Many people think it's right that students help to ...⁶ for their education.

CLARE Sure, I understand that. But I still think people who have to work while they're at school are at a disadvantage.

BOB Well, most American ...⁷ are looking for someone with experience. They think working while you're at school helps young people to learn important job-related skills.

CLARE Oh, come on, Bob! Filling supermarket shelves and cooking burgers are skills, are they?

BOB That's not what I meant. I'm talking about real ...⁸ that are important for all jobs. Things like getting to work on time – I mean, if you can't organize your ...⁹ then you're not ready to work yet. Part-time jobs teach you how to work well with other ...¹⁰ too.

3 LOOKING AT THE TEXT

Do the following tasks.

1 List three objections that Clare has to school students taking part-time jobs.
2 Say why Bob is sceptical about Clare's point that some young people have to take a job just to live.
3 Explain why American employers think that working your way through school or college is an advantage.
4 Describe the misunderstanding that Clare and Bob have about 'job-related skills'.

4 WORKING WITH WORDS

A Find the English equivalents of these German phrases in the interview in exercise 2. They are in the same order.

1 Keine Ursache!
2 darauf ankommen
3 über die Runden kommen
4 recht haben
5 Wirklich?
6 eigentlich nicht
7 Ich bitte dich!
8 nicht so weit sein

B Use two of the English words or expressions you found in exercise A to complete these cartoons.

C Complete Susan Barton's description of her job with words from the box.

afternoons | brochures | busy | careless | customers | interesting | main job | parents | pay | part-time | plenty | work

Hi. My name's Susan Barton and I'm 17. I'm still at school, but I have a ...[1] job at a travel agency in the town centre. I ...[2] there for three hours on Wednesday, Thursday and Friday ...[3], and four hours on Saturday mornings, from 8:30 to 12:30. That makes 13 hours in all, which my ...[4] say is more than enough.
My ...[5] is to make sure that there are always enough ...[6] in the racks, and that they are all correctly sorted. That doesn't sound much, but in fact there's ...[7] to do. Some people are so ...[8]. They often look at brochures and then put them back in the wrong rack – if they put them back at all, that is! Now that I have been there for a few months, I also sometimes help the assistants to deal with ...[9] and answer the phone when we're ...[10]. As I like people, I find that more ...[11] than just looking after brochures, of course. And the ...[12] is good – £5.50 an hour! I certainly can't complain about that, can I?

5 SPEAKING

A Work with a partner. Take it in turns to ask each other questions about your part-time jobs. Use the language below to help you.

Do you have a part-time job?	*Yes, I do. / No, I don't.*
What do you do?	*I'm a bartender/cashier/shelf-stacker/waiter/...* *I give private tuition.* *I help in an old people's home / at a filling station / ...*
How long have you had it?	*I've had it for* (+ Zeitraum: *six weeks, three months).* *I've had it since* (+ Zeitpunkt: *last February, summer 2008).*

B Now discuss someone you know who has a part-time job.

Does ... have a job?	
What does he/she do?	*He's/She's a ...*
How long has he/she had it?	

6 LOOKING AT GRAMMAR: PRESENT PERFECT

Form

Your boss ***has asked*** *you to clean the floor.* *A lot of students* ***have taken*** *part-time jobs.*	*have/has* + 3. Form **regelmäßig:** *have/has* + 3. Form auf *-ed* **unregelmäßig:** *have/has* + unregelmäßige 3. Form: siehe S. 245
Ellie ***has not / hasn't found*** *a job yet.*	**Verneinung:** *not* unmittelbar hinter *have/has*
Have you *answered the questions honestly?*	**Fragen:** Austausch von Subjekt und *have/has*

Gebrauch

I can't come to work. I ***have hurt*** *my hand.* *Jane isn't here. She****'s gone*** *to the bank.*	**ohne Zeitangabe** für Situationen/Ereignisse, die **noch andauern** oder deren Auswirkungen noch in der Gegenwart spürbar sind
Have *you* ***ever been*** *to the USA, Holly?* *I****'ve never had*** *a part-time job.* *Casey* ***hasn't answered*** *my email* ***yet****.* *Part-time work among the over-16s* ***has increased*** *a lot* ***since the 1990s****.* *Maddy* ***hasn't stopped*** *eating* ***all day****.*	mit **Zeitangaben für die ganze Zeit bis jetzt** wie *ever* (jemals), *never, yet, still, for* (+ Zeitraum), *since* (+ Zeitpunkt)
Ellie ***has just found*** *a job at a boutique.* *I****'ve been*** *to the cinema a lot* ***recently****.*	mit **Zeitangaben für die (aller)letzte Zeit** wie *just, recently*

⚠ **Beachten Sie** die Stellung der Adverbien:
The film has ***just*** *started.*
The bus has ***already*** *left.*
I have ***never*** *been to New York.*
They ***(still)*** *have* ***not*** *finished the job* ***yet****.* ⚠ (immer) noch nicht

A Put the verbs into the correct form of the present perfect. Be careful about negatives and questions.

1 The students *have already arrived*[1] (*already* + *arrive*). In fact, they ...[2] (*already* + *be*) here for an hour.
2 The mechanic ...[1] (*repair*) the car and he ...[2] (*wash*) it as well.
3 The men ...[1] (*not start*) work yet. ...[2] (*you/tell*) them what to do yet?
4 I ...[1] (*not see*) Ben since yesterday. I hope he ...[2] (*not take*) the day off again.
5 The boss ...[1] (*ask*) twice if we ...[2] (*finish*) this job yet.
6 I ...[1] (*not be*) here long. I ...[2] (*only* + *live*) in Atlanta for two weeks.
7 ...[1] (*Benny/clean*) the floor yet? I ...[2] (*ask*) him to do it several times.
8 ...[1] (*you/meet*) our new part-timer yet? He ...[2] (*just* + *start*) here.

B Complete the sentences with *for* (period of time: *for two years*) or *since* (point in time: *since 3 o'clock*).

1 I haven't watched TV ... last weekend.
2 Have you seen Carey ... she got back from Georgia?
3 I haven't seen Sharon ... months.
4 Amy has worked here ever ... we opened.
5 Jack hasn't spent any time with his family ... years.
6 Holly has worked here ... a month now.
7 I haven't seen Ann ... she started her part-time job.
8 Kenny has only lived in England ... a few weeks.

C Look at the pictures. Use the present perfect to say what has *just* happened.

1 finish
The film *has just finished.*

2 leave
Mum and Dad ... for work.

3 send
Ed ... a text message.

4 switch on
Susan ...

5 clean
The boys ...

6 begin
The news ...

7 MANAGING SITUATIONS

Sie möchten jemandem auf Englisch sagen, dass ...

1 ... Sie seit sechs Monaten einen Nachmittagsjob haben.
2 ... Sie gerade eine E-Mail geschrieben haben.
3 ... Holly nie für Geld gearbeitet hat.
4 ... Familie Carter seit zwei Jahren in Deutschland wohnt.
5 ... Sie seit drei Wochen in einem Computergeschäft arbeiten.
6 ... Ihr/Ihre Freund/in gerade angerufen hat, um Ihnen seine/ihre Ankunftszeit (*time of arrival*) zu sagen.

1 City lights

FOCUS

1 Read the quotation. Explain how this statement could be true.

'The strange thing about New York City is that you feel as though you've been there before, even if you've never set foot in the US.' Simon Gage, Introduction to *Out Around New York*

2 Look at photos A–F and match them to places 1–6.

1 Brooklyn Bridge
2 Central Park
3 Grand Central Terminal
4 the Chrysler Building
5 the Empire State Building
6 the Statue of Liberty

A

B

C

D

E

F

3 Work with a partner. Think of films that show these places. Use the ideas below to help you talk about the films.

A	*I think the Empire State Building*	*features appears*	*in King Kong.*
B	*Oh, you mean that (famous)*	*scene, sequence,*	*don't you? The one where King Kong climbs to the top and catches planes in his hand.*

4 Say which place in New York you would most like to visit and why. Use the list from exercise 1 or your own ideas.

A Personal perspectives

BEFORE YOU READ

A Compare and contrast the two photos opposite. Use the language below to help you.

One photo shows a city scene, whereas the other one ...

In the picture on the right,	*there are a lot of* *we can see lots of*	*cars, while in the ...*

B Scan the emails quickly and find out who they are to and from.

> Lesen schwieriger Texte: Skimming S. 160

1 LOOKING AT THE TEXTS

A Read the emails and do these activities.

> Lesen schwieriger Texte: Close reading S. 160

1 Put emails A–D in order from 1 to 4.
2 Name the places in the photos. Match the writer and reader of the emails to the photos.
3 Find the state of Oregon and the city of New York on the map at the back of the book. Say roughly how far Ricky and his family travelled when they moved.
4 Put the following events in the order that they happened.
   a Ricky meets Lucy.
   b The family move to their new apartment.
   c Ricky goes to a party with his new friend.
   d Ricky and his family travel to New York.
   e The family look for a place to live.
   f The family move into a hotel.
   g The family see Manhattan from the top of the Empire State Building.

B Say what you think.

1 Compare the endings of the emails.
2 Work out what is probably happening with Ricky and Lucy.
3 What are your views on this kind of change in this particular situation?

C Compare urban and rural life.

1 Imagine a New York family moving to Silver Creek. Say how they might feel about their new home. Use these phrases and adjectives to help you.
Compared with NY, life here is much more ...
The people are a lot less ...

calm | enjoyable | exciting | fast | friendly | fun | gentle | intense | interesting | noisy | pleasant | quiet | relaxed | slow

2 Say if you would prefer to live in New York or in Silver Creek. Use phrases like these.
Personally, I would prefer to live in ...
I think life there would be (much) more ... than life in ...
I don't think life there would be as ... as life in ...

A

Dear Sue

I still miss you as much as ever – more, in fact! I've been checking out flight prices on the internet, and they're less expensive than I thought. Pretty soon, I promise, I'll be back in Silver Creek with you.

I still can't get used to this city. It's just too fast, too loud. The people too. Out on the street, they seem to power-walk all the time – except when they stop to yell at each other!

Yesterday, we went up the Empire State Building, and the view was really something. The downtown Manhattan skyline just blows you away.

Must run. We're going to check out some places to live.

Lots of love

Ricky

B

Dear Sue

Well, I'm starting to like New York a lot more than before. They say it's the most exciting place in the world, and maybe it really is. Music, sport, cinema, festivals – you name it, and it's here.

I start at JF Kennedy High next week, and that's scary. But I met a girl called Lucy in the elevator – she lives two floors down – and we got talking. Turns out Lucy's at JFK, and she's going to be a senior too. She's going to introduce me to everyone, and that's great.

There's a lot more to tell you, but I have to stop now. I'm going to a party with Lucy.

All best wishes

Ricky

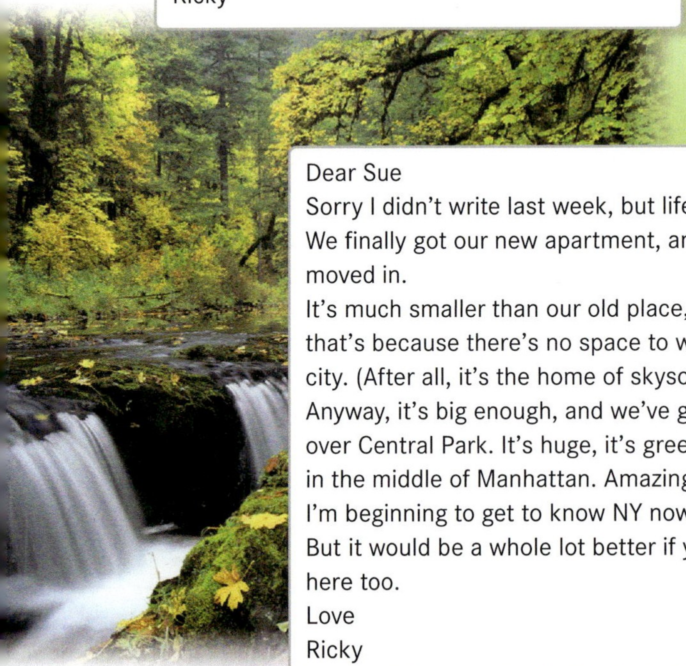

C

Dear Sue

Sorry I didn't write last week, but life was busy. We finally got our new apartment, and last week we moved in.

It's much smaller than our old place, but I guess that's because there's no space to waste in this city. (After all, it's the home of skyscrapers, isn't it?) Anyway, it's big enough, and we've got great views over Central Park. It's huge, it's green and it's right in the middle of Manhattan. Amazing.

I'm beginning to get to know NY now, and it's OK. But it would be a whole lot better if you could be here too.

Love

Ricky

D

Dear Sue

I still can't believe what's happening. A week ago, I was still in the best place in Oregon, with the best girl in the world.

And now what? The forest and falls are gone, and I'm stuck in this non-stop nightmare of noise. Even up here on the 17th floor of our hotel, you still hear the traffic 24-7. What are Mom and Dad thinking of, coming to work in New York?

All I want is to get back home to see you. I miss you more than anything in the world. Write soon.

I love you to bits! XXXOOOXXXOOO

Ricky

(438 words)

2 WORKING WITH WORDS

A Explain the words and expressions from their context.

1 Email A, line 12: ... the view was **really something**.
2 Email A, line 13: The downtown Manhattan skyline just **blows you away**.
3 Email B, line 6: ... – **you name it**, and it's here.
4 Email D, line 6: ... you still hear the traffic **24-7**.

B Find words and phrases in the emails that mean the same as the following.

Email A	Email B	Email C	Email D
1 shout	4 frightening	6 suppose	9 waterfalls
2 city-centre (adjective)	5 lift	7 exactly	10 never-ending
3 have a look at		8 much	

C Now use some of the words from exercise B to complete these sentences.

1 We have a ... apartment ... opposite the new shopping mall.
2 I once got stuck in the ... of a skyscraper – it was really ...
3 I ... we could ... the new art exhibition tonight – we have no other plans.

3 BUILDING SKILLS: LISTENING

1 6 **A Listen for general understanding. Listen to Part 1 and complete the statements.**

> Das Hörverständnis üben S.162

1 The speakers are probably ...
  a New York City tourist guides.
  b tourists in New York.
  c presenters on a TV travel programme.

2 The speakers are talking about ...
  a how to get to New York.
  b what to see and do in New York.
  c what to eat in New York.

1 7 **B Listen for detail. Listen to Part 2 and take notes. Copy the table on the right. Then cross out the things that are not suggested and write down times for those that are.**

Suggestion	*Time needed*
~~*the Chrysler Building*~~	...
the Empire State Building	*1 hr*
Broadway	...
Times Square	... 4 hrs
Central Park	... 4-5 hrs
helicopter ride	... 5 min for 69 $
the Statue of Liberty	... some hours
the Staten Island Ferry	... 1 1/2 hrs

4 WRITING

Write Sue's reply to Ricky's last email.

1 Start with your greeting:
Dear ...
2 Paragraph 1: Refer to Ricky's email, and say how you felt when you received it.
Well, I got your email. And when I read it, I have to say I felt ...
3 Paragraph 2: Say how you feel about the relationship and what has happened to it.
Thinking about our relationship now, it seems to me that ...
4 Paragraph 3: Say what you think should happen now.
I'll tell you what I think should happen now. I think ...
5 Use one of Ricky's endings.

B The bigger picture

BEFORE YOU READ

A Look at the map. Do these activities.

1 Try to match the six famous places shown in Focus to numbers 1–6 on the map. Check your answer with the Key on page 159.

2 Say how a) a German immigrant in 1900 and b) a German tourist today might reach the centre of New York.

B The main title of the text on page 40 is 'A Bite of the Big Apple'. Say what you think the text might be about.

C Look at the sub-headings. Which of the following could the text be from?

an encyclopedia entry on New York
a novel about life in New York
a tourist guidebook about New York

A Bite of the Big Apple

Coming to New York

When you come from the airport on a sunny day, the distant towers of Manhattan shine magically. Closer, as you cross the river, the great skyline still takes your breath away, even though you know it from a thousand films.

As you begin exploring 'the Big Apple', you soon realize that it is many cities in one. For a start, New York is far more than Manhattan. Famous though this is, it is only one of five boroughs. There are also the Bronx, Brooklyn, Queens and Staten Island. Together, they cover the shores and islands of the Hudson and East Rivers and New York Bay.

Every borough has a different look and feel to it, and within each there are neighbourhoods, all with their own characteristics and sense of community.

The melting pot

Much of the city's variety comes from its many cultural and racial traditions. In the 19th century, the city drew millions of Irish, German, Italian and other immigrants from Europe. And since then the waves of immigration have never stopped. After World War II, they came from Latin America and the Caribbean, and then from eastern Europe and Asia. In fact, 36% of today's New Yorkers were born abroad.

New York has also always attracted Americans from all over the country - people who want to make it in the big city.

The effects are everywhere. There are street festivals for everything from Chinese New Year to St Patrick's Day. In Queens, for example, you will hear a hundred different languages. As for food, you will find every dish under the sun in New York City.

The city that never stops

By the late nineteenth century, Manhattan was becoming quite crowded. With typical energy, New York began to use the newly-invented steel-frame construction to build streets to the sky. The skyscraper was born.

This energy is famous and has made New York the city that never sleeps. It has also made it a world leader in many areas, including banking, fashion, advertising, media, the arts and information technology. And, of course, NYC is the shopping capital of the world!

However, there have been hard times, too. The worst was in the 1970s. Drugs and crime were taking over, taxpayers were moving out and the city was nearly bankrupt. But, as always, the city came back stronger than ever.

The terrorist attacks of 9/11 of course brought more hard times, and another bad period of business failure and unemployment followed. The huge new 'Freedom Tower' will soon replace the former World Trade Center, as a symbol of the city's recovery.

(441 words)

1 LOOKING AT THE TEXT

A Copy the mind map and add to it from the text and the map.

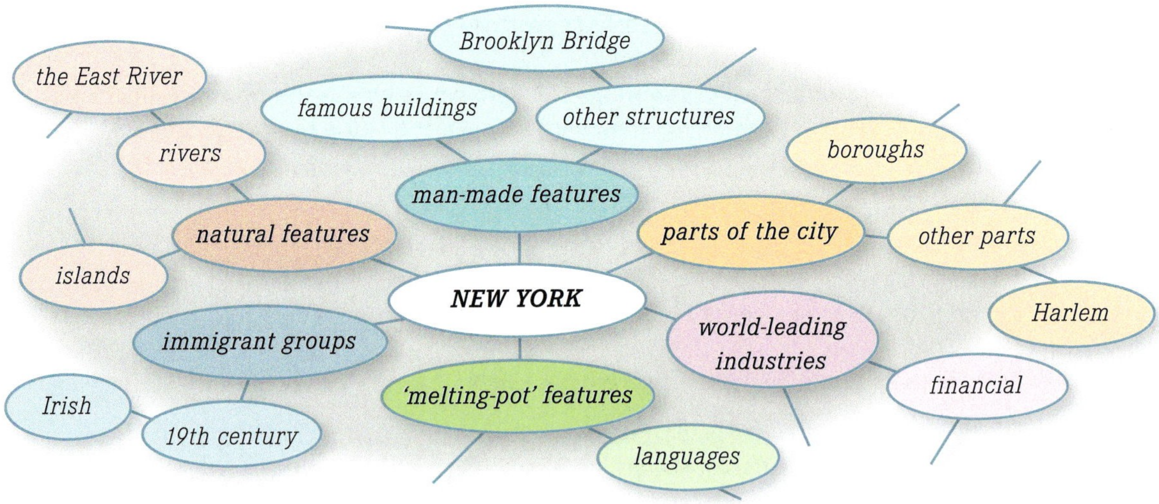

B Complete the sentence beginnings 1–5 by adding a sentence part from the first box and an ending from the second.

> Lesen schwieriger Texte: Scanning S. 161

1 Manhattan is the most famous part of New York, ...
2 The city has many cultural traditions ...
3 It has always attracted not just people from around the world, ...
4 When construction with steel became possible, ...
5 Through its huge energy, ...

... this soon led to the birth of ...
... because of the non-stop ...
... but also people from ...
... but it is only one of ...
... the city now leads the world ...

... every part of America itself.
... in many aspects of life.
... the skyscraper in crowded Manhattan.
... the five city boroughs.
... waves of immigrants.

C Write out the sentences from exercise B as a short summary. Start like this:

Manhattan is the most famous part of New York, but it is only one of the ...

2 WORKING WITH WORDS

Copy and complete the table with a) words from the text, and b) other words that you know. (Check your dictionary if necessary.)

> **TIP** When you collect words like this, you get two, three or even more words for the price of one!

Verb	*Noun*	*Adjective*
differ	*difference*	...
immigrate	...	
...	*attraction*	...
...	...	*sleepy*
...	...	*leading*
...	...	*informative*
strengthen	...	...

3 BUILDING SKILLS: USING YOUR OWN WORDS

> **TIP** When you do comprehension tasks that require writing, you need to use your own words as much as possible. To help you do this, you can often use different grammatical forms of the words in the text, as in the table on page 41.

A Match the following phrases/sentences 1–5 to sentences in the text with the same meaning. Explain in German how the sentences in the text have been changed.

1 2nd paragraph: ... just one of the five city boroughs.
2 4th paragraph: ... the non-stop waves of immigrants.
3 5th paragraph: ... people from every part of America itself.
4 7th paragraph: This soon led to the birth of the skyscraper.
5 8th paragraph: The city now leads the world in many aspects of life.

B Rewrite the sentences using the words in brackets in the correct form.

1 One great attraction to visitors is the city's huge energy. (*attract*) *One thing that greatly ...*
2 Many parts of NY differ amazingly. (*difference*) *There are amazing ...*
3 NY leads the financial centres of the world. (*leading*) *NY is the ...*
4 This book has a lot of information about NY's history. (*informative*) *This book is ...*
5 Over the last two centuries, large numbers of people continued to immigrate to America. (*immigration*) *Over the last two centuries, large-scale ...*

4 PLANNING A VISIT

A Work with a partner. You have won a competition and the prize is a two-day visit to New York for you and your partner. Follow these steps to plan your visit.

1 Make a list of all the things that you would both like to see and do. You can look back through the Unit for ideas. (Don't worry about money: there's nothing to pay!)

I'd really like to ...	*I've always wanted to ...*

2 Decide how much time you think you need for each thing on your list.

We'll probably need about (one) hour to ...	*We'll definitely take at least ...*

3 If you have too much for a two-day visit, decide which things not to do/see and why.

It'll be better to ... *It'll take too long to ...* *So I'd prefer to ...*	*It'll be more interesting ...* *There isn't enough time to ...* *I'd rather ...*

4 Work out a timetable for your visit.

First, let's ...	*Then, we can ...*

B Together, report your plans to the class. Try to use these words and phrases.

On the (first) day, we're going to ... | In the (afternoon), ... | First of all, ... | Then ... | Next, ... | After that, ... | Afterwards, ... | Finally, ...

C Further options

1 PLANNING A DAY OUT

Students Martin and Kristal have just one free day in New York – Sunday, November 18 – and they want to do all of these things:

> go to a 'ball game' and see one of NY's great baseball sides;
> take in a big Broadway show - something with lots of music;
> experience some really American music, which could be jazz, country, gospel or blues.

Do these tasks.

1 Work out a plan for the day which allows Martin and Kristal to do everything.
2 Shows are expensive in NY, so find out how they can get cheap tickets.

The Baseball lineup

Home / Away

	Thu 15	Fri 16	Sat 17	Sun 18	Mon 19	Tue 20	Wed 21
ny	No game	No game	No game	Lions 1pm Fox	No game	No game	No game
JETS	No game	No game	No game	Steelers 4:05pm CBS	No game	No game	No game
	No game	Islanders 7pm FSNY	Flyers 7pm FSNY				Penguins
NY	Penguins 7:30pm FSNY	Devils 7pm FSNY	No game				

Seats for a song

Rush tickets to Broadway and Off Broadway shows for as little as $20 apiece. Go to the theater's box office on the day of the performance (most open at noon) and wait in line. Some sell rush tickets early, others an hour before curtain. Many shows also offer discounted rates for students and seniors.

Discount tickets available for same-day performances through the Theater Development Fund/TKTS on W 46th St between Broadway and Eighth Ave – Mon–Sat 3–8 p.m.; Wed, Sat 11 a.m.–6 p.m.; Sun 11 a.m.–4 p.m.

The Farnsworth Invention *Music Box Theater, W 45th St between Broadway and Eighth Ave $51.50 –$201.50. Tue 7 p.m.; Wed 2 p.m., 8 p.m.; Thu, Fri 8 p.m.; Sat 2 p.m., 8 p.m.; Sun 3 p.m.* Television heavyweight Aaron Sorkin *(The West Wing)* returns to the stage, but with his eye still fixed on the small screen. His new period drama concerns the 1928 invention of the electronic television by high-school boy genius Philo T. Farnsworth.

♫ ***Mamma Mia!*** *Winter Garden Theater, 1634 Broadway at 50th St. $62.75–$251.50. Wed 2 p.m., 8 p.m.; Thu, Fri 8 p.m.; Sat, Sun 2 p.m., 8 p.m. 2 hrs 30 mins. One intermission.* Almost two dozen hits from the '70s pop sensation ABBA form the spine of this worldwide smash. As a delivery system for pop-

2 WRITE AN EMAIL

Write to an old English friend. Follow these steps.

1 Paragraph 1: Ask how your friend is and thank him/her for the last email/postcard/letter and for all the news. Apologize for taking a while to reply.
2 Paragraph 2: Begin with: *Guess what!* Explain the competition in B4 (page 42) and your prize.
3 Paragraph 3: Describe your plans for the trip (include the big 'sights' and some events above - or anything else you like).
4 Paragraph 4: Write a short closing paragraph (see Ricky's emails on page 37 for ideas).

D Grammar checkpoint

1 COMPARISON OF ADJECTIVES

> Grammar summary S. 178

A **Work with a partner. Choose a city from below and find it on the map at the back of your book. Do not tell your partner the name of your city!**

City	Approx population	City	Approx population	City	Approx population
New York	8.0 million	Houston	2.0 million	Seattle	570,000
Los Angeles	4.0 million	Phoenix	1.4 million	Washington D.C.	560,000
Chicago	3.0 million	San Francisco	750,000	Miami	380,000

B **Give your partner some clues about your city. Which one is it? Can he/she guess?**

A It's bigger than ..., but it isn't as big as ...
B That means you're talking about either ... or ...
A And it's farther south than ..., but it isn't as far south as ...
B Well, in that case, you mean ..., don't you?
A That's right. Now it's your turn. / No sorry. You'd better try again.

2 COMPARATIVES AND SUPERLATIVES

> Grammar summary S. 178

A **Look at *Top Holiday* magazine's survey of New York bus tours. Then read the junior reporter's comments and correct his five mistakes.**

Tour details

	Length of tour	Cost	Departures
Big Apple Tours	2hr 50min	$25.00	Every 30 minutes
City Sights	1hr 50min	$22.00	Every hour
Central Experience	2hr 40min	$30.00	Every two hours

Visitors' opinions

	How interesting?	How helpful?	Value for money
Big Apple Tours	*****	**	****
City Sights	**	*	**
Central Experience	****	***	***

City offers the shortest tour of the three companies. At $22.00, the tour is cheaper than Big Apple's but more expensive than Central's. With departures every hour, it provides the least frequent service of all. Visitors feel that the tour itself is more interesting than Big Apple's and less interesting than Central's. They also say that the company is the most helpful of the three. Overall, they feel that the City tour is better value for money than the Central tour.

B **Now write a similar paragraph to compare Big Apple Tours with City Sights and Central Experience.**

Advertising

FOCUS

1 Advertising never leaves us alone. Where have you seen or heard advertisements in the last 24 hours? What sorts of advertising were they?

brochures | classified, full-page or panel adverts in magazines/newspapers | leaflets | online pop-up/banner ads | posters | product placements (in films or TV programmes) | radio/TV commercials | sponsorship advertising (on football shirts, etc.)

2 What do you think of the adverts above? Use adjectives like these.

annoying | boring | clever | disgusting | funny | glamorous | shocking | silly | strange

3 The aims of advertising vary – for example, to present products, promote brands or to make the public think. What do the adverts above do?

A Personal perspectives

BEFORE YOU READ

Look at the photo, the style of the magazine page and scan the article to decide the probable age range of the target audience: 12–15, 16–24 or 25–35. Give reasons for your choice.

Every week, DO IT! magazine's Ben Starr talks to young people in great jobs who have great futures. This week, Ben meets Lisa Scott at the fast-growing advertising agency *iMAGE iMPACT*.

BEN *Lisa, what brought you to iMAGE iMPACT's online creative team?*

LISA *Well, while I was studying ICT at college, I designed a website for the volleyball team I played for. We were doing well in the national league, so we had lots of hits on the site. We also had a sponsor - SportStyle. They got their name on our shirts, and we got financial help. Then I added a simple game to the website. Visitors to our website pressed number keys to make a player jump and return the ball. Of course, SportStyle's name was on the player's shirt. They loved the whole website - and we got extra money.*

BEN *What happened then?*

LISA *After college, I became a freelance website developer, but I wanted something more. One day, I was looking at job ads on the internet when I saw that 'something'. iMAGE iMPACT were expanding their online creative team, and they wanted someone like me.*

BEN *So you applied for the job. And I guess the interview went well.*

LISA *Yes, and the volleyball website also helped, of course, so here I am. We're still only a small group in the Creative Design Department, but online advertising is the part of the whole business that's now growing the fastest.*

BEN *Where does Creative Design fit in?*

LISA *Well, let's start at the beginning. A potential client needs a campaign for a new product and invites several agencies, including us, to 'pitch' for the contract. One of our account managers visits the client to discuss their needs and then becomes the bridge between the client and us. Together, we and the accounts manager work out the key campaign concept. Then we, the 'creatives', produce the magic words and images that will sell the product.*

BEN *Let's say you win the pitch. What happens then?*

LISA *We get the green light to develop the concept into a full campaign. That's when the media planners also become very important They're the people who decide exactly what media to use when, and how much. We could launch the campaign with a first run of TV commercials, for example, followed by online advertising.*

BEN *And what are you working on at the moment?*

LISA *Right now, I'm having real fun with a campaign for a new online travel agency. I'm using characters from the TV commercials to create a travel game that takes you on journeys to dream destinations right round the world.*

BEN *Well, thank you, Lisa. It's clear that this job really suits you – it's your own dream destination!*

(458 words)

1 LOOKING AT THE TEXT

A Read the text carefully. Choose the best answer or answers.

1 *SportStyle* loved ...
   a the finished website that Lisa produced.
   b playing games with website visitors.
   c Lisa's game and having their name on the player's shirt.

2 *iMAGE iMPACT* wanted a designer ...
   a to join their online creative team.
   b to produce innovative magazine adverts.
   c who could create an online advertising team.

3 Business at *iMAGE iMPACT* is ...
   a declining slightly.
   b fairly stable.
   c rising rapidly.

4 Lisa is now ...
   a working on a campaign for a travel agency.
   b developing a new online travel game.
   c travelling to destinations that she has always dreamed about.

B This flow chart shows how an advertising campaign is set up. Copy and complete it with information from the text. Use the simple present, and leave out unnecessary words, e.g. *a, an, the.*

STEP 1 *Potential client invites agencies to pitch.* →	*STEP 2* ... →	*STEP 3* ... →	*STEP 4* ... →	*STEP 5* ... →	*STEP 6* ... →	*STEP 7* *Agency launches campaign.*

C Which of these typical agency jobs – if any – might be right for you? Why? Discuss with a partner using the words and phrases below.

account manager | creative | IT support staff member | media booker (booking commerical slots, e.g. TV) | media planner | PA (personal assistant) to a senior manager

(I think) I'd find *I'd (probably) find*	*being a (creative)* *the job of (account manager)*	*(very) enjoyable.* *(quite) stressful.*
That's (probably) because *(I think) that's due to the fact that*	*I (don't) like ...* *I'm (quite/not very) good at ...*	

2 BUILDING SKILLS: DESCRIBING A PROCESS

Look back to exercise 1B. Now write a summary of the process in full sentences. Use these connectors.

First (of all), ... | Then ... | Next, ... | After that, ... | Following that, ... | Finally, ...

3 WORKING WITH WORDS

A Copy and complete the table.

B Complete the *iMAGE iMPACT* advert that Lisa saw. Use words from the table.

	Verb	*Noun (thing)*	*Noun (person)*
1	...	*design*	...
2	...	*development*	...
3	...	*interview*	...
4	...	*management*	...
5	*sponsor*	*sponsorship*	...
6	*supply*	*supply*	...

http://www.

iMAGE iMPACT is a fast-developing, London-based advertising agency. We are expanding our online creative team and urgently require an innovative ...[1].
For further information and an application form please visit our website at www.image-impact.co.uk or call Human Resources ...[2] Helen Troy on 020-1946583. The closing date for applications is 28th February, and we expect to ...[3] candidates between 10th and 14th March. All shortlisted candidates will be asked to ...[4] examples of their work.

4 CULTURE CHECK: FORMS OF ADDRESS

Email

Dear Ms Scott,
Thank you for your application for the new position in our online creative team. I am pleased to invite you for an interview on 12th March at 2 p.m. Please confirm that you are able to attend on this date and bring some recent examples of your work with you.
I look forward to meeting you.
Best wishes,
Mandy Carr

Email

Dear Lisa,
I am very pleased to offer you the position in our online creative team. Please reply by 28th March to confirm whether you would like to accept the post. Then we can organize contracts, etc.
I look forward to working with you!
Best regards,
Mandy Carr
P.S. Please do call me Mandy – we are pretty informal here!

Read the correspondence between Mandy Carr and Lisa Scott. Decide the following.

1 When and why were these emails written?
2 What rules does the writer follow? Who can/cannot suggest using first names?
3 In the same situations in Germany, what forms of address would people use?

> **INFO**
>
> **1** *Mr*, *Mrs* and *Ms* are the usual formal titles used when dealing with clients, customers and senior colleagues. *Ms* is used for all women, whether they are married or not.
> **2** In many companies, staff use first names with each other, even between junior and senior staff. This may seem very informal, but it is not and has nothing like the closeness of the German *du*.
> **3** As in Germany, changing from formal style to first names must come from the senior person, e.g. here, from Mandy Carr to Lisa Scott.

5 SPEAKING

Discuss things that you should and should not do before and during an interview.

B The bigger picture

1 10 BEFORE YOU READ

A **Where does this text come from?**

B **Look at the heading. Say what you understand by the word 'Forum'.**

http://www.

FOCUS Forum

JOIN TODAY'S DISCUSSION: 'We're swimming in a sea of advertising'

Rob, London, UK

Dear FOCUS Forum
It's more true to say that we're drowning in a sea of advertising! And what's so terrible is that it tries to control our minds.
We just have to ignore all the thousands of adverts around us as much as we can. For example, when commercial breaks come on, it's time to make coffee. Even better, I often record programmes and my DVD recorder automatically cuts the commercials.

Lucy, Melbourne, Australia

Dear FOCUS Forum
Rob is far too negative. We live in a very rich society that offers lots of choices. And advertising tells us about those choices. Think of it as a public information service! Personally, I also love ads. They're lively and fun. So lighten up, Rob!

Julia, Seattle, United States

Dear FOCUS Forum
Like Rob I hate living in a sea of advertising, but I know that we can't escape from the advertisers so easily. Just think of the branded entertainment on our screens. With all that product placement, programmes like House Wars are really extended commercials! For example, the competing families always go to the same store for their building supplies.
And then there's online viral advertising, too. This often comes as a game, and it passes from friend to friend by email. And then the product appears on every screen. It spreads around the world like a virus.
'Word of mouth' agencies that pay people to talk up a product at parties or in online chatroom discussions are just another sort of viral advertising.
So while I really dislike traditional advertising, I prefer it to the new methods. At least you know it when you see it, and you can always change channel or turn the page. Viral advertising is often harder to recognize.

Peter, Johannes-burg, South Africa

Dear FOCUS Forum
Unlike Julia, I think viral advertising is good because it's cheaper than traditional forms of advertising. I must admit, I do worry about those billions of dollars that traditional advertisers spend. What's more, advertising makes us buy more than we need, so we're using global resources more wastefully than ever. We should spend the money on something more useful – more hospitals, for example.

Sally, Toronto, Canada

Dear FOCUS Forum
Poor Peter! He just doesn't understand. Advertising adds a bit to costs, but it helps keep the whole global economy going. Without it, sales drop, companies collapse, jobs disappear, the economy fails, and we all go back to the Middle Ages! Is that what we want? Are we mad enough to do that?

(409 words)

1 LOOKING AT THE TEXT

A Read for information.

1 List four different forms of advertising that are mentioned in the text.
2 Which are traditional 'hard sell' methods and which more modern 'soft sell' techniques?

B Use the information from the forum to decide which person made each comment. Read the speech bubbles 1–5 and match them to the photographs A–E.

1 *I enjoy watching ads on the TV! And I often buy things that I see in adverts.*

2 *Yes, advertising makes products a bit more expensive, but we would have so many problems without it.*

3 *People don't understand how much advertising there is around them – it's everywhere. We just can't escape from it!*

4 *I don't let advertising influence me. I do everything I can to avoid it. People should make their own choices.*

5 *What about the impact on the environment? Just think of all the raw materials that are used up to produce the things we buy.*

A Rob, 17

B Lucy, 15

C Julia, 20

D Peter, 18

E Sally, 20

C Explain one point of disagreement between each pair.

Use these connectors in your answers.

but | whereas | while | By contrast | However | On the other hand

1 Rob and Lucy 2 Rob and Julia 3 Julia and Peter 4 Peter and Sally

EXAMPLE *Rob says that there is far too much ..., while Lucy feels that advertising ...*

D Say what you think.

1 Name some adverts that you like or dislike and say why.
I love/hate that new advert for ... because ...

2 In Focus Forum there are five different opinions on advertising. Which do you agree/disagree with? Use these phrases:
I totally/partly agree/disagree with ... when he/she says/suggests that ...
Personally, I think that ... is exaggerating.
It seems to me that ... is giving a one-sided view.
In my opinion, ... has got it about right.

2 LISTENING

1 11 **A Listen and do the activities.**

> Das Hörverständnis üben S.163

Mandy Carr, Creative Director at *iMAGE iMPACT*, is explaining a well-known advertising technique to a group of students.

1 Listen and make notes. Note what AIDA stands for.
2 Say why this advert is a good example of AIDA.

3 BUILDING SKILLS: ANALYZING CHARTS

> Interpretation von Grafiken, Diagrammen und Tabellen S.168

A Match the chart types a–c to their names 1–3.

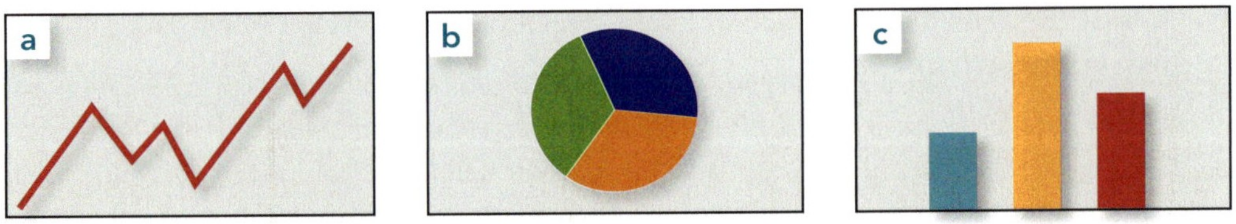

1 bar chart 2 line graph 3 pie chart

> **TIP** Charts show statistical information in a way that is easy to understand. When you give presentations, try to use suitable charts to support your explanations.

B Here are some useful words for describing graphs and statistics. Use them to describe what is happening in A–F.

verb +	*adverb*	*adjective +*	*noun*	*verb +*	*adjective*
rise	*rapidly*	*rapid*	*rise*	*be*	*flat*
increase	*sharply*	*sharp*	*increase*	*remain*	*steady*
grow	*steadily*	*steady*	*growth*		
fall	*gradually*	*gradual*	*fall*		
decrease	*slowly*	*slow*	*decrease*		
decline	*slightly*	*slight*	*decline*		

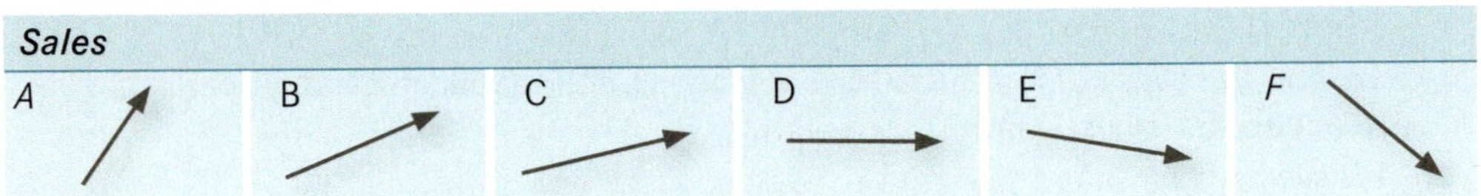

EXAMPLE *In A, sales increased sharply.*

C Read and do the activities.

Tony Lee, *iMAGE iMPACT*'s Finance Director, is describing some company sales trends.

1 Look at the chart, read what Tony Lee says, and decide whether he is talking about total sales or TV sales.
2 Say which five years he is talking about.

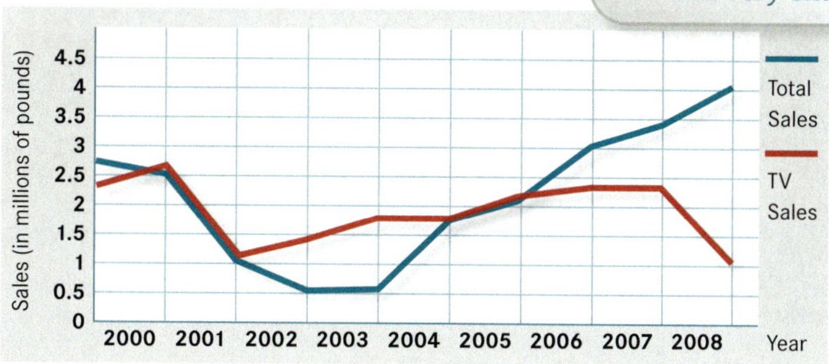

4 WRITING

A Look at the timeline and read about the development of *iMAGE iMPACT*. Then do the activities.

1 Find information that comes from the above chart for *Total Sales*.
2 Compare the style of the notes and the full text. Find:
> words that the full text adds;
> full forms of the abbreviations that are used in the notes.

iMAGE iMPACT Timeline	
2000	Mandy Carr & Tony Lee build up new agency – small office, SE London; worldwide dot-com crash begins > immediate problems.
2001	Crash hits global advertising industry v hard. *iMAGE iMPACT* nearly goes bankrupt.
2004	Company slowly recovers, M&T decide to start online advertising & hire new staff to help.
2006	Online creative team win several important contracts. *ii* moves to bigger offices.
2007	*ii* wins 2 important advertising industry awards > new clients & business.
2008	Further expansion of online advertising. Most other areas also grow, but not TV.

The development of *iMAGE iMPACT*
While Mandy Carr and Tony Lee were building up their new agency in a small office in South-East London in 2000, the worldwide dot-com crash began. This led to immediate problems. Sales grew quite slowly that year. Then, in 2001, the dot-com crash hit the global advertising industry very hard. Sales fell ...

B Continue the story using the information in the timeline. You can use these intensifiers in your writing.

quite | fairly | very | extremely

C Further options

1 ANALYZING AN ADVERTISEMENT

Work with a partner to write a short analysis. First, find a good advert that uses the AIDA formula. (The advert can be in German or English.) Your analysis should explain the following:

- what the advert is for
- where it comes from
- who it is aimed at (the target audience)
- how it works (using the AIDA formula - see page 51)
- how well it works, particularly with its target audience and why you both like it

2 ANALYZING THE CONSTRUCTION OF ADVERTISEMENTS

Work with a partner, and analyze the advert on the right. Think about:

- what first draws the eye to the advert
- the arrangement of images, colours and words
- the message that the advertiser wants to get over to you
- how the images, colours and words support that message

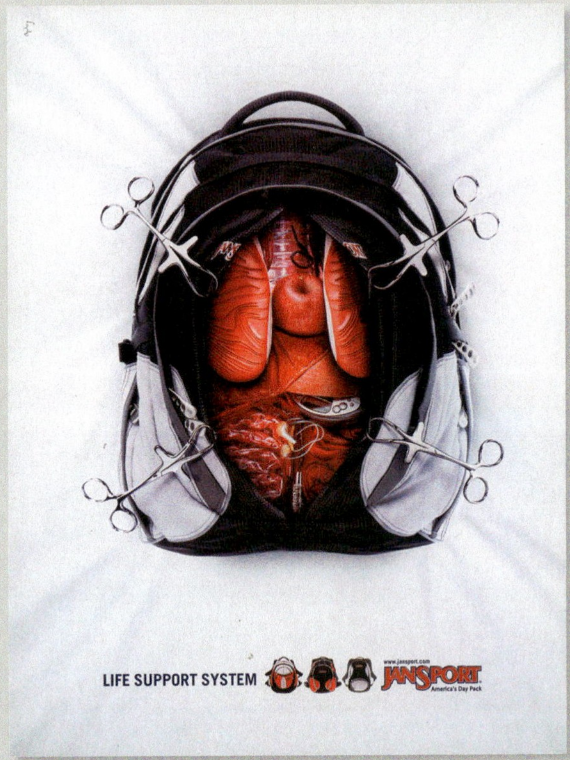

3 CONSTRUCTING AN ADVERTISEMENT

Work with a partner. As creatives, work out an advertising concept for a new product, for e.g. a new high-tech mobile phone, a glamorous range of fashion accessories or a special event.

- Agree on your target audience.
- Work out a message that will attract that audience.
- Develop the images, colours and words that will support that message.

4 PRESENTING YOUR PITCH

Work with another pair - they are your agency's clients. Take turns to pitch to each other. Explain your concept and your choice of image and words. Try to persuade them that your ideas would make a great campaign.

5 WRITING A FOCUS FORUM COMMENT

> Eine Stellungnahme (*comment*) schreiben S.170

In exercise 1D (page 50) you discussed other comments in FOCUS FORUM. Now write your own comment about advertising in today's world.

D Grammar checkpoint

1 PAST PROGRESSIVE

> Grammar summary S. 181

At 6 p.m. everybody at *iMAGE iMPACT* was still working. Use the past progressive to say what they were doing. Add any missing words.

1 Lisa Scott (test) / new online game / SkyTravel.com.
Lisa Scott was testing her new online game for SkyTravel.com.
2 Mandy Carr (prepare) business plan / next year.
3 Tony Lee and his assistant (study) / latest sales figures.
4 Media planners (discuss) / new campaign.
5 Carrie, the senior account executive, (call) / client / America.

2 PAST PROGRESSIVE AND SIMPLE PAST

Fill in the gaps with the past progressive or simple past. (Use the past progressive when both tenses are possible.)

Lisa has worked very long hours for months now, without any holidays.Yesterday, for example, she *was still working*[1] (still work) at 7.00, and she *finally finished*[2] (finally finish) at nearly 7.30.

While she ...[3] (walk) past an electrical store on her way to the bus stop, something on the TV screens in the window ...[4] (catch) her eye. They ...[5] (show) the new SkyTravel commercial! Then she ...[6] (remember): this ...[7] (be) the first day of the campaign.

At home, Lisa ...[8] (put) a curry in the microwave and ...[9] (turn on) the TV. She ...[10] (see) the commercial again. The people in it ...[11] (have) a wonderful time on a golden beach under a blue sky. 'And why not me, too?' Lisa ...[12] (ask) herself. The company owes me two weeks' holiday!'

While she ...[13] (eat) her curry, Lisa ...[14] (log on) to SkyTravel. She ...[15] (get) really excited when she ...[16] (find) cheap holidays available in Ibiza. Two minutes later, she ...[17] (talk) on the phone to her friend Alice about dates. Later, she ...[18] (think), 'Our commercial must be pretty good: it even worked on me!'

3 RELATIVE CLAUSES

> Grammar summary S. 184

Form complete sentences by putting together one sentence from 1–5 and one from a–e. Make them into one sentence by adding *who, which* or *that*.

1 Rob (be) the person
Rob is the person who tries to ignore and avoid advertising.
2 Lucy and Sally (be) the ones
3 Viral advertising (be) a new type of advertising.
4 Rob (use) a DVD recorder
5 There (be) programmes like *House Wars*

a It (cut) the commercials.
b They clearly (support) advertising.
c They (be) really just long commercials.
~~d He (try) to ignore and avoid advertising~~.
e It (work) by spreading from person to person, often by email.

4 RELATIVE CLAUSES AND CONTACT CLAUSES

Copy and complete the slogans. Add *who*, *which* or *that* where necessary. If not, write *X*.

1 STARWAYS – a film *X you'll never forget.*
2 AIR-WISE – the people ... get you there
3 HOME GYM – for a personal trainer ... you can trust
4 PRO-VIT – the vitamins ... doctors recommend
5 LOOKS – for fashion ... won't break the bank
6 RANGER XF – the car ... the whole world's waiting for
7 SAT-PAK – the satnav system ... beats them all

Focus on Success

ALLGEMEINE AUSGABE – THE NEW EDITION

Von: Clarke, David/ Macfarlane, Michael.

Schülerbuch
(1. Halbjahr 2009) ca. 208 S. KT
[Best.-Nr. 202273]
978-3-06-020227-0 ◐ ca. € 23,95

Workbook mit herausnehmbarem Lösungsschlüssel
(1. Halbjahr 2009) ca. 48 S. KT
[Best.-Nr. 202300]
978-3-06-020230-0 ◐ ca. € 8,95

CDs
(3) Ca. 150 Min.
(1. Halbjahr 2009)
[Best.-Nr. 202683]
978-3-06-020268-3 ◇ ca. € 29,95

SOZIALES – THE NEW EDITION

Von: Clarke, David/ Macfarlane, Michael/ Willams, Steve/ Williams, Steve.

Schülerbuch
(1. Halbjahr 2009) ca. 260 S. KT
[Best.-Nr. 202290]
978-3-06-020229-4 ◐ ca. € 23,95

Workbook mit herausnehmbarem Lösungsschlüssel
(1. Halbjahr 2009) ca. 64 S. KT
[Best.-Nr. 202713]
978-3-06-020271-3 ◐ ca. € 8,95

CDs
(3) Ca. 150 Min.
(1. Halbjahr 2009)
[Best.-Nr. 202744]
978-3-06-020274-4 ◇ ca. € 29,95

TECHNIK – THE NEW EDITION

Von: Clarke, David/ Macfarlane, Michael.

Schülerbuch
(1. Halbjahr 2009) ca. 272 S. KT
[Best.-Nr. 202281]
978-3-06-020228-7 ◐ ca. € 23,95

Workbook mit herausnehmbarem Lösungsschlüssel
(1. Halbjahr 2009) ca. 64 S. KT
[Best.-Nr. 202706]
978-3-06-020270-6 ◐ ca. € 8,95

CDs
(3) Ca. 150 Min.
(1. Halbjahr 2009)
[Best.-Nr. 202737]
978-3-06-020273-7 ◇ ca. € 29,95

WIRTSCHAFT – THE NEW EDITION

Von: Benford, Michael/ Clarke, David/ Macfarlane, Michael.

Schülerbuch
(1. Halbjahr 2009) ca. 260 S. KT
[Best.-Nr. 202751]
978-3-06-020275-1 ◐ ca. € 23,95

Workbook mit herausnehmbarem Lösungsschlüssel
(1. Halbjahr 2009) ca. 64 S. KT
[Best.-Nr. 202775]
978-3-06-020277-5 ◐ ca. € 8,95

CDs
(3) Ca. 150 Min.
(1. Halbjahr 2009)
[Best.-Nr. 202768]
978-3-06-020276-8 ◇ ca. € 29,95

ZU ALLEN AUSGABEN

Handreichungen für den Unterricht mit CD-ROM
(1) Einzellizenz
(1. Halbjahr 2009) ca. 168 S. KT
[Best.-Nr. 202676]
978-3-06-020267-6 □ ◇ ca. € 18,95

European Union